영어 문장의 모든 것

이것이 구문이다!

저자 이종현

머리말

영어는 위치어이고 영어 문장을 보며 각 단어들이 어떠한 이유로 그 자리에 위치했는지만 정확하게 파악할 수 있어도 편입, 수능 등 공인 영어 시험에 나오는 모든 문장들은 해석이 가능합니다. 그런데 시중에 많은 교재들은 이런 기본과 본질을 설명하지 않고 마치 무슨 비기인 것처럼 책을 써서 학생들을 현혹시킵니다. 각 문장의 위치를 정확하게 파악하는 공부를 하지 않는다면 설사 책에서 본 비슷한 모양을 다른 문장에서 본다고 할지라도 절대 해석할 수 없는데 이걸 설명하지 않은 채 그저 학생들을 현혹시키기 위한 구문 책들을 보며 이 책을 만들게 되었습니다.

여러분들은 이 **이것이 구문이다!** 책에서 영어 해석의 본질을 공부하게 될 것입니다. 본질이라고 해서 복잡할 것 같지만 전혀 복잡하지 않습니다. 본래 본질이 가장 단순한 법입니다. 그 본질만을 파악하고 암기해서 수능 문장을 가장 빠르고 정확하게 해석하게 만드는 길을 제시해드리겠습니다. 지금까지는 듣지 못했고 지금까지는 뚫리지 않던 영어문장이 시원시원하게 뚫리는 경험을 하게 될 겁니다.

영어는 절대로 어려운 언어가 아닙니다. 다만 여러분들이 다른 곳에서 괜히 어렵게 들었기 때문에 어려운 것입니다. 이 **이것이 구문이다!**가 여러분들의 영어의 길에 있어서 큰 전환점이 되어줄 것입니다. 그리고 이를 바탕으로 원하는 꿈과 목표를 꼭 한번 성취해보시길 바랍니다.

이 교재 학습법

우리가 영어 문장을 해석할 때 가장 큰 문제는 문법적 구조에 대해 전혀 생각하지 않고 대충 아는 단어를 짜깁기해서 해석을 맞춰본다는 것이다. 그러다보니 정확한 해석이 어렵고 전부 애매하게 해석이 될 때가 많다. 이를 해결하기 위해 만든 이 책은 공인 영어시험에 나올법한 모든 문장 패턴을 다 담았다. 따라서 여기에 있는 문장들의 패턴들만 정확하게 학습하고 익혀놔도 어떤 영어 문장을 봤을 때 처음 본다는 느낌 없이 확실하게 해석하는 것이 가능할 것이다. 이 책 문장들에 대한 정확한 공부법을 한번 알아보자.

1 문장을 구조분석하기

먼저 문장을 구조분석을 한다. 이 구조분석을 할 땐 해석하려고 하지 말고 문장의 구조만 나눈다는 마음으로 보면 된다. 해석을 하기 전에 정확한 문장구조를 확실하게 파악하기 위한 연습이다.

2 구조분석한 문장을 직독직해로 해석해보기

구조분석한 문장을 직독직해로 해석해본다. 이 땐 어순을 생각하지 말고 그냥 끊어진 그대로 해석한다는 마음으로 직독직해를 한다.

3 직독직해로 해석한 문장을 의역으로 바꿔보기

이제 직독직해로 해석한 문장을 의역으로 해석해본다. 직독직해로만 해석할 경우 무슨 말인지 이해가 안될 수 있다. 따라서 직독직해로 쓴 문장이 무슨 말인지를 확실하게 받아들이기 위한 고민을 해보면 된다.

4 해설지 확인 + 동영상 강의

책 뒤편에 해설지를 보면 지금 말한 공부법대로 정확하게 구조분석과 해석을 써놓았다. 따라서 해설지를 확인해보면 된다. 그리고 이 이외에 혹시 완벽하게 공부를 하며 필요한 포인트를 전부 정리하고 싶다면 www.ibroun.com에서 동영상으로도 학습을 할 수 있게 강의를 촬영해두었다. 혼자 공부해도 충분하지만 동영상 강의로 정리하면 완벽하게 정리할 수 있을 것이다.

Contents

Part 2. 복잡한 구문 총정리

기초 개념 총정리

품사와 성분의 차이

품사

단어의 역할을 8가지로 나눠서 8품사라고 한다. 즉 품사=단어의 역할이다.
그런 품사에는 **명사, 대명사, 동사, 형용사, 부사, 전치사, 접속사, 감탄사** 등이 있다.

성분

성분은 흔히 문장의 성분이라고 하고 이는 문장에서의 위치에 대한 개념이다. 따라서 품사와 혼동되면 안된다. (성분 = 문장에서의 위치). 이런 성분에는 **주어, 동사(서술어), 목적어, 보어, 수식어구** 등이 있다.

형용사와 부사의 차이

형용사

단어의 뜻이, -ㄴ, ~의, ~할 등으로 끝나는 단어를 형용사라고 한다. 이런 형용사는 문장에서 명사를 꾸며주는 역할(명사 수식), 보어 역할(동사 뒤에 위치)을 한다.

부사

단어의 뜻이 ~하게, ~하여 등으로 끝나는 단어를 부사라고 한다. 보통 부사는 형용사 뒤에 ly를 붙인 형태가 많다. 이러한 부사는 문장에서 동사 수식, 형용사 수식, 다른 부사 수식, 문장 전체 수식 등의 역할을 한다. 부사는 문장에서의 위치가 자유롭다.

구와 절의 차이

우리말에서도 '잘생긴 남자아이'라고 하면 잘생긴과 남자아이를 두 개의 단어로 보지 않고 묶어서 하나의 의미단위로 보는 것처럼 영어에서도 여러 단어를 묶어서 하나의 의미단위, 즉 하나의 단어처럼 보는 경우가 있다. 이를 구와 절이라고 한다.

① **구와 절의 공통점** : 둘 다 여러 단어를 묶어서 그게 마치 하나의 단어처럼 쓰인다는 것은 공통점이다. 그래서 하나의 품사를 가질 수 있다.(명사/형용사/부사)

② **구와 절의 차이점** : 절은 접속사 + S V(문장) 의 형태이다. 즉 문장을 한 단어처럼 쓴 것을 절이라고 하고, 그냥 문장 형태가 아닌데 여러 단어를 묶어서 하나로 쓴걸 구라고 한다.

* 전명구는 형용사구 or 부사구다!

구의 종류는 여러 가지인데 그 중 전치사 라는 품사 뒤에 명사가 오게 되면(전치사 + 명사) 그 둘은 묶어서 하나의 의미 단위로 쓰게 된다. 그래서 하나의 품사도 가지게 되고, 이러한 전치사 + 명사 의 형태는 문장에서 형용사 또는 부사처럼 쓰인다.

영어 문장은 5가지의 형식으로 나눠진다! (1~5형식)

이렇게 여러 성분들이 모여 문장을 이루고, 그 문장은 특징에 따라 5형식으로 나눌 수 있다.

① S + Vi + (부사/부사구/부사절)

② S + Vi + S.C

③ S + Vt + O

④ S + Vt + I.O + D.O

⑤ S + Vt + O + O.C

주어의 종류 총정리

명사구의 종류

① 명사 후치수식 주어

＊명사 + 형용사구의 형태와 해석법

1) [명사 + (전명구)] + V : [~에 있는 '명사'] + V

2) [명사 + ing] + V : [-ing하는 '명사'] + V

[명사 + p.p] + V : [p.p된/진 '명사'] + V

3) [명사 + 형용사(+ 전명구/to v)] + V : [~해서/~하다니(~하는걸보면) '형용사'한 '명사'] + V

[명사 + to v ~] + V : [~할 수 있는/~하기 위한 '명사'] + V

ex The ability to v ~ : ~할 수 있는 능력
The capacity to v ~ : ~할 수 있는 능력
The willingness to v ~ : 기꺼이 ~하려는 것

＊명사 + 형용사절의 형태

1) [명사 + who/which/that v] + V ~ : [V한 '명사'] + V

[명사 + whom/which/that s vt ~] + V : [S가 V한 '명사'] + V

[명사 + S Vt ~] + V : [S가 V한 '명사'] + V

2) [명사 + where/when/why s vt ~] + V : [S가 V한 '명사'] + V

[명사 + that s v(완전한 문장)] + V : [S가 V한 '명사'] + V

[명사 + 전치사 + which/whom + S V ~] + V : [S가 V한 '명사'] + V

[명사(A) + whose + 명사(B) + V/S Vt ~] + V : [V한 '명사(B)'를 지닌/S가 V한 '명사(B)'를 지닌 '명사(A)'] + V

② 명사 후치수식이 아닌 명사구 주어

[To v ~] + V : [v하는 것은] + V

[V-ing ~] + V : [-ing하는 것은] + V

③ 명사절 주어

[That S V ~] + V : [S가 V하다는 것] + V

[What V ~] + V : [V하는 것/무엇이 V하는지] + V

[What S Vt ~] + V : [S가 V하는 것/무엇을 S가 V하는지] + V

[Which + V ~] + V : [V하는 것/무엇이 V하는지] + V

[Which + S Vt ~] + V : [S가 V하는 것/무엇을 S가 V하는지] + V

[Who V ~] + V : [누가 V하는지] + V

[Whom S Vt ~] + V : [누구를 S가 V하는지] + V

[Where S V ~] + V : [어디에서 S가 V하는지/S가 V하는 장소] + V

[When S V ~] + V : [언제 S가 V하는지/S가 V하는 시기] + V

[Why S V ~] + V : [왜 S가 V하는지/S가 V하는 이유] + V

[How S V ~] + V / [How 형/부 + S V ~] + V : [어떻게 S가 V하는지/S가 V하는 방법] + V / [얼마나 ~하게 S가 V하는지] + V

[What/Which 명 V ~] + V : [어떤 '명사'가 V하는지] + V

[What/Which 명 S Vt ~] + V : [어떤 '명사'를 S가 V하는지] + V

[Whose + 명 + V ~] + V : [누구의 '명사'가 V하는지] + V

[Whose + 명 + S Vt ~] + V : [누구의 '명사'를 S가 V하는지] + V

[Whether S V ~] + V : [S가 V인지 아닌지] + V

[Whatever/Whichever V ~] + V : [V하는 무엇이든] + V

[Whatever/Whichever S Vt ~] + V : [S가 V하는 무엇이든] + V

[Whoever + V] + V ~ : [V하는 누구든] + V

[Whomever + S Vt ~] + V ~ : [S가 V하는 누구든] + V

[Whatever + 명 + V ~] + V ~ : [V하는 어떤 '명사'든] + V

[Whichever + 명 + S Vt ~] + V ~ : [S가 V하는 어떤 '명사'든] + V

memo

Part 01

문장의 5형식

UNIT 1 1형식

1형식 문장 : S + Vi + 수식어구

01 1형식 문장이 길어지는 이유 : 수식어구 때문! [부사(구)(절)]

02 1형식 동사의 종류 : 자동사!

＊자동사란?

목적어가 필요없는 동사 → 주어가 행동하는 것에 대한 대상이 필요 없음.

03 대부분의 동사는 자동사와 타동사 2가지 의미를 다 지니고 있다!

＊ '있다'라고 해석하는 동사

lie, stand, sit, be동사

＊ 이외의 대표적인 1형식 동사

live - Vi : 살다 / Vt + O(life) : 삶을 살다
count - Vi : 중요하다/ Vt + O : ~를 세다
matter - 명사 : 물질, 일, 문제 / Vi : 중요하다
exist - Vi : 존재하다
respond - Vi : 반응하다 + to 명사
go - Vi : 가다
go away : 사라지다
go after : ~를 쫓아가다
go on : 계속 하다
pay - Vi : 이익이 되다, 효과가 있다 / Vt : 지불하다
work - Vi : 일하다, 노력하다, 작동하다, 작용하다, 효과가 있다

＊ There is/are + 명사 : ~가 있다

문제풀이 기출문장을 통한 확인

1. The environmental adversities actually contribute to their longevity.

2. The new information can contribute to a completely different perspective in finding a solution, thus producing the Aha! Experience.

문제풀이 기출문장을 통한 확인

3. When the habitat disappears, a vast number of species disappear as well.

4. Growth is always at the edges, just outside the boundaries of where you are right now.

문제풀이 기출문장을 통한 확인

5. Often, however, regulations on meeting reporting requirements do not work adequately, as the Enron scandal in 2001 clearly illustrates.

6. There were no vocalizations that I was aware of that might indicate Sarah was distressed by Harper's thievery, nor that Sheba was trying to appease any distress.

문제풀이 기출문장을 통한 확인

7. Scientific and professional expertise often relies on a particular type of knowledge which is limited to utility and rationality considerations.

8. The Health Management Program lasts for six weeks and consists of three different components: Daily Targets, Walking Plans, and Eating Plans.

문제풀이 기출문장을 통한 확인

9. When there is a discrepancy between the verbal message and the nonverbal message, the latter typically weighs more in forming a judgment.

10. The train arrived at my destination ten minutes early, which was perfect, as I was due to present my new idea to the company at 10 a.m.

UNIT 2 2형식

2형식 문장 : S + Vi + S.C(주격 보어)

01 2형식 문장 : S + Vi + S.C(주격 보어)

* 보어는 주어와 같은 대상이거나, 주어의 상태를 나타내준다. (S = S.C)
  보어 자리에 올 수 있는 품사 : 명사, 형용사, 명사구, 명사절, 형용사구 (-ing, p.p도 가능)

02 대표적인 2형식 동사 : be동사 (is/am/are/was/were)

→ S는 S.C 이다라고 해석

* 주요 2형식 동사 총정리

되다
become, go, get grow, turn, run, fall, come, make

~인 채로 있다
remain, stay, stand, keep, lie, hold, rest

~인 것 같다
seem, appear

~임이 입증되다
prove, turn out, come out

오감동사
look, sound, taste, smell, feel

* 가주어/진주어
It + Vi + C + to v ~ / 명사절

문제풀이 기출문장을 통한 확인

11. An old teapot which has lost its lid becomes an ideal container for a bunch of roses picked from the garden.

12. A tool may be awkward to use and inefficient, or possibly even dangerous — a hammer is a good example. However, it may be so familiar to so many people that they have become accustomed to its disadvantages and may be able to use it very effectively, despite the disadvantages and inconvenience.

문제풀이 기출문장을 통한 확인

13. Small changes in the sensory properties of foods are sufficient to increase food intake.

14. These are among the basic questions that were addressed at the first world meeting on the environment, attended by more than 100 world leaders and 30,000 other scientists, newspeople, and citizens concerned.

문제풀이 기출문장을 통한 확인

15. Comparison with the inferior is self-enhancement at work. But what happens when the only available comparison target we have is superior or better off than we are?

16. Hence, raising awareness of children from a very early age about the particular characteristics of SNS and the potential long-term impact of a seemingly trivial act is crucial.

문제풀이 기출문장을 통한 확인

17. Disease, as a sanction against social misbehavior, becomes one of the most important pillars of order in such societies.

18. Natural preference for foods appears to be specific evolved mechanisms, designed to deal with the adaptive problem of food selection, and coordinate consumption patterns with physical needs.

문제풀이 기출문장을 통한 확인

19. Indeed, print-oriented novelists seem doomed to disappear, as electronic media and computer games are becoming more influential.

20. Falling in love is like being wrapped in a magical cloud. The air feels fresher, the flowers smell sweeter, food tastes more delicious, and the stars shine more brilliantly in the night sky.

문제풀이 기출문장을 통한 확인

21. You look at the trees and the mountains through windows that are wet with rain from a storm, and everything looks shapeless and out of focus.

22. So the only thing you can do is try to fail faster so that you can move onto the next idea.

문제풀이 기출문장을 통한 확인

23. The good news is that it's never too late to start building up muscle strength, regardless of your age. Ideally, though, it's best to start in your mid-forties when muscle mass starts to decline significantly.

24. It is easy to find examples of correlations which are far more systematic than could occur by chance and yet which it would be absurd to treat as evidence of a direct causal link.

문제풀이 기출문장을 통한 확인

25. Parental enthusiasm for head-up motor accomplishments from their infants is not at all misplaced, for they are, indeed, milestones of development.

26. Politics cannot be suppressed, whichever policy process is employed and however sensitive and respectful of differences it might be. In other words, there is no end to politics. It is wrong to think that proper institutions, knowledge, methods of consultation, or participatory mechanisms can make disagreement go away

문제풀이 기출문장을 통한 확인

27. One of my dreams was to become a photographer. That dream came to an abrupt halt in a photography class. There was no denying in the other students' pictures that they were far more talented than I was.

28. People are much more concerned about catching the ball than throwing it. What this demonstrates is that it's equally as important to the success of the exercise that the person you're throwing to catches the ball as that you are able to catch the ball.

문제풀이 기출문장을 통한 확인

29. The essential argument here is that the capitalist mode of production is affecting peasant production in the less developed world in such a way as to limit the production of staple foods, thus causing a food problem.

memo

UNIT 3 3형식

3형식 문장 : S + Vt + O(목적어)

01 3형식 문장 : S + Vt + O(목적어)

* 목적어는 주어가 동사의 행동을 했을 때 영향을 받는 대상이다.(대상어)

02 목적어의 해석은 '~을/를'으로 해석이 된다.

03 목적어 자리에 올 수 있는 품사 : 명사, 대명사, 명사구, 명사절

* 목적어 자리에 올 수 있는 명사구/절의 형태

- 명사구 : to v, v-ing, 명사 후치수식

- 명사절 : that s v
  what / which v / what / which s vt
  who v / whom s vt
  where s v
  when s v
  why s v
  how s v / how 형/부 s v
  what / which / whose + 명사 + v / s vt
  if/whether s v
  whoever v / whoever s vt
  whatever / whichever v / s vt

* 주로 명사절을 목적어로 취하는 3형식 동사

think, know, say, believe, suppose, insist, mean, explain, argue 등

* 동사 뒤에 to v가 오는 것과 ing 오는 것에 따라 의미가 달라지는 동사들

stop, try, regret, forget/remember, mean

- stop to v : ~하기 위해 멈추다 / stop -ing : ~하는 것을 멈추다
- try to v : ~하기 위해 노력하다 / try -ing : ~하는 것을 시도하다
- regret to v : ~하게 되어 유감이다 / regret -ing : ~했던 것을 후회하다
- forget/remember to v : ~할 것을 잊다, 기억하다
- forget/remember -ing : ~했던 것을 잊다, 기억하다
- mean to v : ~할 의도이다 / mean -ing : ~하는 것을 의미하다

* 3형식 문장의 수동태

S + Vt + O -> O + be p.p by S

문제풀이 기출문장을 통한 확인

30. Subscriptions account for almost 90 percent of total magazine circulation. Single-copy, or newsstand sales account for the rest.

31. One wonders whether our children's inherent capacity to recognize, classify, and order information about their environment — abilities once essential to our very survival — is slowly evolving to facilitate life in their increasingly virtualized world.

문제풀이 기출문장을 통한 확인

32. One may wonder if literary fiction is destined to become an old-fashioned genre to be preserved in a museum like an extinct species.

33. Geniuses don't necessarily have a higher success rate than other creators; they simply do more — and they do a range of different things.

문제풀이 기출문장을 통한 확인

34. We could have seen something many times before, but as the result of having new skills or competence, we discover new or different aspects of that object.

35. I have had the opportunity to look over your poems, and I feel that they show considerable promise, despite your youth and lack of experience in this genre.

문제풀이 기출문장을 통한 확인

36. Industries are competitively changing their businesses into e-businesses, and thus the demand for the required workforce is expected to grow.

37. Finally, local residents may feel that marketing process reduces their identities to mere commercial transactions, and they may believe they sacrifice what is unique and special about their place.

문제풀이 기출문장을 통한 확인

38. No matter how hard you may try to produce an objective paper, the fact is that every choice you make as you write is influenced to some extent by your personal beliefs and opinions. What you tell your readers is truth, in other words, is influenced, sometimes without your knowledge, by a multitude of factors: your environment, upbringing, and education; your attitude toward your audience; your career goals; and your ambitions for the paper you are writing.

39. We've emphasized that hereditary factors are critical in determining which children can look forward to being outstanding, and perhaps even elite, athletes. However, the effects of genetics are never absolute because genes do not operate in isolation. We cannot undervalue the influence of the environments in which we live — natural, social, and athletic.

문제풀이 기출문장을 통한 확인

40. People who change do not question whether change is possible or look for reasons they cannot change. They simply decide on a change they want and do what is necessary to accomplish it.

41. Whether their grandchildren have special needs or not, grandparents shouldn't overlook the value of incidental learning experiences.

문제풀이 기출문장을 통한 확인

42. 73 percent of Canadian voters surveyed denied in the strongest possible terms that their votes had been influenced by physical appearance; only 14 percent even allowed for the possibility of such influence.

43. Today the term artist is used to refer to a broad range of creative individuals across the globe from both past and present.

문제풀이 기출문장을 통한 확인

44. When deciding whether to invest in a company, for example, they may take into account the people at the helm; the current and potential size of its market; net profits; and its past, present, and future stock value, among other pieces of information.

45. In addition to protecting the rights of authors so as to encourage the publication of new creative works, copyright is also supposed to place reasonable time limits on those rights so that outdated works may be incorporated into new creative efforts.

문제풀이 기출문장을 통한 확인

46. Supporters of Copyright Act like to defend these increases with tales of starving writers and their impoverished descendants, but in reality the beneficiaries are more likely to be transnational publishing companies.

47. Society, through ethical and economic constraints, exerts a powerful influence on what science accomplishes. At the same time, the results of science have profound, and sometimes unexpected impacts on every human being on earth.

문제풀이 기출문장을 통한 확인

48. Researchers have suggested that maintaining good social relations depends on two complementary processes: being sensitive to the needs of others and being motivated to pay compensation when a violation does occur. In short, maintaining good social relations depends on the capacity for guilt.

49. Organizations with job openings are looking to fill a slot in one area, and they need someone who can jump in right away.

문제풀이 기출문장을 통한 확인

50. The roadside is crowded with locals, and their brains are crowded with local knowledge, but we are too arrogant and embarrassed to ask the way.

51. Bold claims were made by critics of the day who averred that Russian technology wasn't advanced enough to perform an wonderful feat.

문제풀이 기출문장을 통한 확인

52. It's not so much that your memory of last week's lunch has disappeared; if provided with the right cue, like where you ate it, or whom you ate it with, you would likely recall what had been on your plate. Rather, it's difficult to remember last week's lunch because your brain has filed it away with all the other lunches you've ever eaten as just another lunch.

memo

UNIT 4 4형식

4형식 문장 : S + Vt + I.O (간접목적어) + D.O (직접목적어)

01 4형식 문장 : S + Vt + I.O (간접목적어) + D.O (직접목적어)

* 간접목적어는 직접목적어를 받게 되는 대상, 직접목적어는 주어가 주는 물건이다. (4형식 동사는 수여동사)

* 주요 4형식 동사
give, offer, pass, bring, buy, send, teach, show, buy, make, ask

* 직접목적어자리에 that s v가 많이 오는 4형식 동사 (이 땐 무조건 4형식)
tell, convince, inform, notify, assure, remind, warn

* 유의할 4형식 동사
1. do + I.O + D.O [good(이익)/ damage(손해)/ harm(피해)]
: ~에게 이익, 손해, 피해를 주다

2. do I.O + a favor
: ~에게 호의를 베풀다

* 3형식같지만 4형식으로 해석하는 동사

1. rob/ deprive (빼앗다)
   rid/ remove/ strip (제거하다) A of B (A에게서 B를)
2. convince, warn, inform, assure, remind, tell + A of B (A에게 B를)
3. provide, supply, present, furnish, endow + A with B (A에게 B를)
4. prevent, prohibit, keep, stop, bar, ban, dissuade, refrain, hinder, inhibit, deter, restrain, discourage + A from B
   : A가 B하지 못하게 하다

* 4형식 문장을 3형식으로 변환

S + Vt + I.O + D.O → S + Vt + D.O + 전치사(to/for/of) + I.O

* 4형식 문장의 수동태

1) 간접 목적어가 주어로 나오는 수동태

S + Vt + I.O + D.O → I.O + be p.p + D.O + (by S)

2) 직접 목적어가 주어로 나오는 수동태

S + Vt + I.O + D.O → D.O + be p.p + 전치사(to/for/of) I.O + (by S)

문제풀이 기출문장을 통한 확인

53. In an open discussion designed to solve problems, the discussion group leader should give group members a chance to make suggestions before making his own.

54. By giving Apocalypse Now a setting that was contemporary at the time of its release, audiences were able to experience and identify with its themes more easily than they would have if the film had been a literal adaptation of the novel.

문제풀이 기출문장을 통한 확인

55. However, we can anticipate that personal growth and performance will progress faster in young, developing athletes who are given mental skills training than in athletes not exposed to MST.

56. Psychologists who study giving behavior have noticed that some people give substantial amounts to one or two charities, while others give small amounts to many charities.

문제풀이 기출문장을 통한 확인

57. I asked my friends what they would do to change the world if they could.

58. Think about the pressure associated with having to convince the other party we are right when we think we are wrong.

문제풀이 기출문장을 통한 확인

59. By giving yourself freedom to follow your intuition, you develop your sensitivity to your inner voice.

60. In 1513, Machiavelli had acknowledged in Il principe that citizens might have a right to ‘think all things, speak all things, write all things,; but insisted that the prince was always equally entitled to deny them this privilege.

문제풀이 기출문장을 통한 확인

61. Experiment and observation provide us with clues, but the clues are cryptic, and require some considerable ingenuity to solve.

62. Human intelligence makes use of very effective pruning techniques that prevent the brain from running in overdrive, attempting to process billions of potential situations of which only one or two might be useful. The expense of this brute computational approach is simply not suited to biological beings. However, what is clear is that the availability of practically infinite mathematical ability, and abundant calculating speed, do result in discoveries that our biological brains have not yet made.

memo

UNIT 5 5형식

5형식 문장 : S + Vt + O (목적어) + O.C (목적격보어)

01 5형식 문장 : S + Vt + O (목적어) + O.C (목적격보어)

02

목적격 보어는 목적어와 같거나 목적어의 상태를 나타내준다.
[2형식에서 주어(S)와 주격 보어(S.C)의 관계와 같다.]

03

목적격 보어에 오는 형태
[명사, 형용사, 분사(-ing/p.p), to be 명/형, as 명/as 형, to부정사, 원형부정사]

1. 목적격보어에 명사가 주로 오는 5형식 동사
call, name + O + O.C(명사) : O를 O.C라고 부르다.

2. 목적격보어에 형용사가 주로 오는 5형식 동사
think, find, believe, keep, leave
① think, find + O + O.C (형용사) : O를 O.C라고 생각하다.
② keep, leave + O + O.C (형용사) : O를 O.C인 채로 두다.
③ believe + O + O.C (형용사) : O를 O.C라고 믿다.

3. 목적격 보어 자리에 as 명/ as 형이 오는 동사

① regard, define, think of, look upon, describe, refer to, imagine, acknowledge, see, view + O + O.C (as 명/형)
: O를 O.C라고 여기다/간주하다.

② consider, deem + O + O.C (명사/ 형용사/ to v/ to be 명,형/ as 명,형)
: O를 O.C라고 여기다/간주하다.

4. 사역동사/준사역동사의 5형식
make, have, let

① make 5형식
- make + O + O.C(동사원형) : O이/가 O.C하게 하다.
- make + O + O.C(p.p) : O이/가 O.C되게/지게 하다.

② have 5형식
- have + O + O.C(동사원형/ing) : O이/가 O.C하게 하다.
- have + O + O.C(p.p) : O이/가 O.C되게/지게 하다.

③ let 5형식
- let + O + O.C(동사원형) : O이/가 O.C 하게 하다.
- let + O + O.C(be p.p) : O이/가 O.C되게/지게 하다.

5. 지각동사의 5형식
see, watch, observe, look at, hear, listen to, feel, notice

① 지각동사 + O + O.C (동사원형/ing)
: O이가 O.C하는 것을 보다/듣다/알아차리다/느끼다 등

② 지각동사 + O + O.C (p.p)
: O이/가 O.C되는/지는 것을 보다/듣다/알아차리다/느끼다 등

6. 일반동사의 5형식

① 소망/의도/기대

want, wish, intend, would like, expect, mean

* mean + O + to v : O이/가 to v하는 것을 의도하다.

② 요청/간청/설득/재촉

tell, ask, advise, urge, beg, persuade, motivate

* ask + O + to v : O이/가 to v하는 것을(하도록) 요청하다.

③ 명령/요구

order, get, cause, force, compel, oblige, command, require

* get + O + O.C(to v/-ing) : O가 O.C 하게 하다.
get + O + O.C(형용사) : O를 O.C하게 만들다.

④ 가능/허가/도움

enable, allow, permit, encourage

⑤ 금지

forbid

* 가목적어/진목적어

- make, find, think, believe, consider, feel + it + 형/명 + to v/that s v

- make + it + 형/명 + to v/that s v
  (~하게 만들다) (~하는 것을)

- find/think/believe/consider/feel + it + 형/명 + to v/that s v
  (~라고 생각하다/생각하다/믿다/여기다/느끼다) (~하는 것을)

* 5형식 수동태

S + Vt + O + O.C → O + be p.p + O.C + (by S)

5형식을 수동태로 만들면 2형식처럼 해석한다.

ex) S + be made + 명/형(be made를 마치 become처럼 해석한다.)
→ S는 ~가 되다.

S + be left/kept + 형용사(be left/kept를 마치 remain처럼 해석한다.)
→ S는 ~인 채로 있다.

S + be regarded/seen/viewed/referred to/thought of/looked upon as 명/형
→ S는 ~라고 여겨지다.

문제풀이 기출문장을 통한 확인

63. Because of his injury, Jim wasn't able to play on the basketball team during the rest of that year, but the coach did make him equipment manager so that he could come and practice.

64. Composers describe their private world through the use of sound. Making such a description concrete and detailed requires not just inspiration but certain practical tools and skills.

문제풀이 기출문장을 통한 확인

65. Medicine comes in lots of different packages. Painkillers in tablet can make your headache go away. Antibiotic cream from a tube can prevent your cuts from becoming infected.

66. Empower people by letting them know that you believe in them and allowing them to take action.

문제풀이 기출문장을 통한 확인

67. For books, there are various filters that help readers distinguish between reliable and unreliable information.

68. As Tom was waiting for a bus, he noticed a blind man trying to cross the street. The traffic was heavy, and it was likely the blind man would get hit, as he was not crossing at a crosswalk.

문제풀이 기출문장을 통한 확인

69. As anyone who has ever watched a parent, a sibling, a spouse succumb to the spreading darkness knows, there is no way to stop the lights from turning off, no way to switch them back on once they've grown dim.

70. The combustion of oxygen that keeps us alive and active sends out by-products called oxygen free radicals.

문제풀이 기출문장을 통한 확인

71. A proportion of agricultural land is left completely uncultivated so that species can gradually colonize it.

72. As we invent more species of AI, we will be forced to surrender more of what is supposedly unique about humans. Each step of surrender — we are not the only mind that can play chess, fly a plane, make music, or invent a mathematical law — will be painful and sad.

문제풀이 기출문장을 통한 확인

73. Because the glow of meteors' burning makes them visible, people often call them shooting stars.

74. We regard butterfly wings as being colorful which are so pretty that many designers always want to use them as their sources.

문제풀이 기출문장을 통한 확인

75. Forcing your children to eat, especially if they don't like what is on the plate, is completely counterproductive.

76. The new bill obliges the public sector to reserve more than a 3-percent share for job applicants aged between 15 and 29 from next year.

문제풀이 기출문장을 통한 확인

77. Knowing the value of your time enables you to make wise decision about where and how you spend it so you can make the most of this limited resource according to your circumstances, goals, and interests.

78. It's utterly possible that new technological breakthroughs will make it possible to find new oil fields faster than we do today, or to pump oil from places that we can't today.

문제풀이 기출문장을 통한 확인

79. There are some people who believe that no one should be trusted. They usually feel this way because their behavior compels others to lie to them. In other words, they make it difficult for others to tell them the truth because they respond rudely or emotionally to people who tell the truth.

80. With the coming of the Industrial Revolution, the social concentration of activities of the public square and indeed the entire public realm has diminished. Technological innovations including the telephone and the Internet combined in the latest cell phone innovations are partly responsible. The automobile has made it possible to travel in virtual privacy and thus withdraw from contact with others in trains, buses, and other forms of public transportation.

문제풀이 기출문장을 통한 확인

81. A round coin is seen as round even when viewed from an angle at which, objectively, it should appear elliptical. In the same way, we see car wheels as round, even though the retinal image is oval when viewed from an angle other than directly from the front..

82. For example, an infant may point to Daddy's chair as a reference to the absent daddy. This type of pointing can be seen as a transition from using pointing as a proto-demonstrative with a temporary meaning to using pointing symbolically with a more permanent meaning.

문제풀이 기출문장을 통한 확인

83. It is helpful to think of sports as an art form — as a performing art. Sports share with other cultural expressions an appeal to the emotions, aesthetics, drama, entertainment, and inspiration. The athlete can be considered an artist with a certain amount of self-expression and spontaneity.

84. Within the philosophical disciplines, logic must be learned through the use of examples and actual problem solving. Only after some time and struggle does the student begin to develop the insights and intuitions that enable him to see the centrality and relevance of this mode of thinking.

정답과 해설 p. 158

문제풀이 기출문장을 통한 확인

85. When I asked a sales person to map his sales performance, he was amazed to see that he had achieved a 5% to 10% annual increase in sales while at his firm.

memo

memo

Part 02

복잡한 구문 총정리

UNIT 1 도치 구문

01

1형식 도치

S + Vi + 전명구 → 전명구 + Vi + S

02

2형식 도치

S + Vi + S.C → S.C + Vi + S

03

3형식 도치

S + Vt + O → O + S + Vt

S + Vt + "   " → "   " + Vt + S/S + Vt

S + Vt + 명사절 목적어 → 명사절 목적어 + Vt + S/S + Vt

5형식 도치

S + Vt + O + O.C → S + Vt + O.C + O

S + Vt + O(형용사절) + O.C → S + Vt + O + O.C + (형용사절)

O + S + Vt + O.C

04

부정어구 도치

Never/ Not/ Hardly/ Rarely/ Scarcely/ Seldom/ Barely/ Little/전 + no + 명/Only + V + S (의문문 어순 도치)

05

So/Nor/neither 도치

S + V ~(긍정문), so + V + S(의문문 어순 도치) → ~도 그렇다

S + V not ~ (부정문), nor + V + S(의문문 어순 도치) → ~도 그렇지 않다

and neither V + S(의문문 어순 도치) → ~도 그렇지 않다

문제풀이 기출문장을 통한 확인

1. More important than success, which generally means promotion or an increase in salary, is the happiness which can only be found in doing work that one enjoys for its own sake and not merely for the rewards it brings.

2. In the center of the room was the strangest lady I had ever seen, sitting at a table.

3. So strong was the emotion that the brain rejected evidence of the continued existence of normal, everyday life that might have eased it.

문제풀이 기출문장을 통한 확인

4. Most helpful to the calm and peaceful atmosphere that the two-year-old child needs but cannot produce for himself/herself is the presence of comforting music, in almost any form.

5. Things we thought we wanted most intensely, we realize, we don't care about.

6. Competition has made possible the enormous material progress of the past 200 years by unlocking the energies of society.

문제풀이 기출문장을 통한 확인

7. The federal government, private research groups, and others collect and provide valuable information and extensive data on many facets of economic life, and the computer has made possible speedier and more sophisticated testing of ideas.

8. We have regarded as natural the body that our parents gave us — a fixed, unchanging fact of nature.

9. Not until they began cultivating tobacco for sale abroad could they finance their activities and develop their country.

문제풀이 기출문장을 통한 확인

10. Lucky lottery winners or other recipients of sudden wealth buy a large house, fancy furniture, a new car, etc. but rarely does the money appear to open the way for a more meaningful, exciting existence.

11. Not only does the 'leaf fish' look like a leaf, but it also imitates the movement of a drifting leaf underwater.

12. Only then can social policies be considered key factors of production, beyond their role as instruments of social protection.

문제풀이 기출문장을 통한 확인

13. As our incomes and material standards rise, so do our expected achievements.

14. The green movement is sometimes criticized for downplaying the cost of going green. Just as food movements have sometimes acted unaware of the difficulty of a working-class family negotiating not only its food budget but also the effect on that budget of the time constraints of working parents, so too did the early environmentalism movement sometimes pay too little attention to the financial effect of environmentally responsible behavior.

문제풀이 기출문장을 통한 확인

15. Truly as the Internet seems global these days, less than half of the world's has access to it.

16. No longer were the shores densely wooded, nor could I see any wildlife anywhere.

17. So popular did they become that the amount of small change minted was inadequate for the demand and the coffeehouses and the houses had to issue tokens that were generally acceptable within the immediate area.

UNIT 2 비교 구문 - 1

01 원급 비교

1. as 형/부 as ~ → ~만큼 ~한/하게

   not so(as) A as B : B와는 달리 A하지 않은/않게

   the same A as B : B와 같은 A

2. 배수사(twice, three times 등) as 형/부 as ~ → ~보다 몇 배 ~한/하게

문제풀이 기출문장을 통한 확인

18. Scientists can lessen bias by running as many trials as possible and by keeping accurate notes of each observation made.

19. At the end of the round of introductions, the students were asked to write down the names of as many other students as they could remember.

문제풀이 기출문장을 통한 확인

20. You are under the false impression that you do not have as many items to pack as you really do.

21. Time itself remains unchanged in the sense that it carries on in the same way as it has for millions of years.

22. The number of researchers per 1,000 people in the EAP in 2007 was twice as large as that in 1999.

UNIT 2 비교 구문 - 2

02 비교급 → the 비교급 ~ the 비교급

1. The 비교급 ~, the 비교급 ~ : ~하면 할수록 더욱 더 ~ 하다

2. (all) the 비교급 + for N/because S + V : ~ 때문에 더욱 ~하다

3. S + V + the + 비교급 + of the two : 둘중에서 더 ~하다

문제풀이 기출문장을 통한 확인

23. The more intelligent you are, the more you may be inclined to consider rapidly many factors before making a decision.

24. When a small butterfly was caught unmercifully in a thornbush, the more the butterfly struggled to free itself, the deeper the thorns cut into its fragile body.

25. The more effectively they communicate that authority, the more secure the child feels, and the better able he is to move away from them toward a life of his own.

문제풀이 기출문장을 통한 확인

26. One of the little understood paradoxes in communication is that the more difficult the word, the shorter the explanation.

27. The higher the economic distance, the higher the resistance for that destination and, consequently, the lower the demand.

28. His morality was severely bruised due to the bribery scandal. And people's anger became all the more intense because he just told lies about the case in a desperate bid to avoid criminal charges.

UNIT 2 비교 구문 - 3

03 최상급 구문(가장 ~한/하게)

1. 최상급 기본 형태 : the + 최상급 + of 복수/in 단수/ever → 가장 ~한

2. 최상급 의미 표현의 문장

① 부정 주어(No ~, Nothing ~) ~ so ~ as ~

② 부정 주어(No ~, Nothing ~) ~ 비교급 + than

③ 비교급 + than + any other 명사

(all) the other + 명사

anyone(thing) else ever

문제풀이 기출문장을 통한 확인

29. There is often no more effective way to help people understand the message than to have it modeled for them by the manager.

30. There are no qualities that an officer must possess as important as loyalty.

31. Nothing is as important as our citizens' safety, so fixing this broken traffic lights should be made a top priority.

문제풀이 기출문장을 통한 확인

32. The report about Africa's potential says that during the past five years, Africa has seen more growth in mobile service subscriptions than any other region in the world.

33. Journeys are the midwives of thought. Few places are more conducive to internal conversations than a moving plane, ship, or train.

34. In this digital age, images are essential units of information, and knowing how to use photography effectively is more important than ever.

문제풀이 기출문장을 통한 확인

35. I was a coward; and the thing I feared more than anything in the world was to break up in the battle and give way to that cowardice.

36. Even the most determined of parents can find it a challenge to encourage their child not to spend too long sitting in front of the television or computer.

UNIT 2 비교 구문 - 4

04 비교급 관용 구문

1. no 비교급 than 구문

① no more than : 겨우(only)

② not more than : 기껏해야(at most)

③ no less than : ~만큼(as much as)

④ not less than : 적어도(at least)

- A is no more B than C (is D) : C가 D 아닌 것처럼 A도 B가 아니다.

  = A is not B any more than C (is D)

- A is no less B than C is D : C가 D인 것처럼 A도 B이다.

2. not so much A as B : A라기보다는 B다

= not so much A, but B

= not so much A, rather B

= not A so much as B

= less A than B

= B rather than A

= more B than A

(Not A, but B와 거의 비슷한 표현!)

3. much / still less / more A → A는 말할 것도 없이

문제풀이 기출문장을 통한 확인

37. Architecture is no more "frozen music" than music is "melted architecture."

38. Organic farmers grow crops that are no less plagued by pests than those of conventional farmers.

39. He is no less diligent than you, but he is not so faithful to his family as you.

문제풀이 기출문장을 통한 확인

40. It is true that there are rules of grammar and syntax just as in music there are rules of harmony and counterpoint. One can no more write good English than one can compose music, merely by keeping the rules.

41. Tolstoy is confident that the artist who sincerely expresses feelings of pride will pass those feelings on to us; we can no more escape than we could escape an infectious disease.

42. A wise person once told me that what's important is not so much the path you're on as the direction you're headed.

문제풀이 기출문장을 통한 확인

43. We learn certain things about the other person not so much from what he says as from how he says it, for whatever we speak we cannot avoid giving our listeners clues about our origins and what sort of person we are.

44. Our nervous system determines the complexity of activities that we are able to perform. Animals with nervous systems similar to a worm's cannot play soccer, much less chess.

memo

UNIT 3 분사 구문

01 (-ing ~), S V ~ : (~하는) S는 V하다

02 (p.p ~), S V ~ : (~되는) S는 V하다

03 (형용사/명사 ~), S V ~ : (~인) S는 V하다

04 (S + -ing/p.p/형/명 ~), S' V ~

: S는 ~하다/되다/이다 (그리고/그래서/그러나/그럴 때) ~하다

05 S V ~, (-ing ~) : S는 V하다 (-ing 하면서/하는채로/ 그리고 ing하다)

S V ~, thus -ing ~ : S는 V하다, 따라서 -ing 하다

06 S V ~, (p.p ~) : S는 V하다, (p.p 되면서 된채로, 그리고 p.p 되다)

07 S V ~, (형용사/명사 ~) : S는 V하다, (~인채로/이면서, 그리고 ~이다)

08 With A B (-ing/p.p/형/명/전명구) ~

: ① A가 B 하면서/되면서/~이면서/~에 있으면서

② A가 B 하는 채로/된 채로/~인 채로/~에 있는채로

③ A가 B 하기 때문에/되기 때문에/~이기 때문에/~에 있기 때문에

문제풀이 기출문장을 통한 확인

45. Recognizing the healing power of humor, many hospitals are starting to take laughing matters seriously.

46. Being careful not to be noticed, he let his eyes trace the figure of her face. Her appearance was simply enchanting.

47. Asked about the most and least trustworthy people in our society, most of them answered professors are the most trustworthy and politicians are the least trustworthy group in society.

문제풀이 기출문장을 통한 확인

48. Given your experience and expertise, I believe you would be an ideal person to speak to them.

49. In doing so, the scientist reverses his drive toward mathematical exactness in favor of rhetorical vagueness and metaphor, thus violating the code of intellectual conduct that defines him as a scientist.

50. These new technologies have revealed that many things can produce infrasound, from earthquakes and thunderstorms to trains and underground explosions, thus making possible the warning of earthquakes and the monitoring of underground nuclear-explosion tests.

문제풀이 기출문장을 통한 확인

51. The making of this requires the mutual agreement of two or more persons or parties, one of them ordinarily making an offer and another accepting.

52. Suddenly, the plane was in the middle of the storm, jumping and swinging in the darkness, the rain crashing down on the windows with incredible violence.

53. Jaisalmer is the only fortress city in India still functioning, with one quarter of its population living within the walls.

문제풀이 기출문장을 통한 확인

54. With nearly eighty percent of mothers of school-age children in the work force, millions of children are on their own between 3.p.m and 6 p.m., the hours when youth are most likely to commit crime or be victimized by it.

55. There was no one in sight but a girl of about twelve, with her eyes covered with bandage, who was being led carefully between the flower beds by a little boy. She stopped, and evidently asked who it was that had come in, and he seemed to be describing me to her.

문제풀이 기출문장을 통한 확인

56. Speaking of marrying creativity and business, I've discovered that a rock star and a brain surgeon have something in common. It's not that either one would be particularly good at the other's craft (and I'm not sure which crossover would produce the more disastrous results), but rather that each one is capable of performing his craft brilliantly, and generating huge sums of money, without the need for any financial skills.

57. Furthermore, given the time and money required to get a PhD and its uncertain economic returns, it is clear that most of us pursue an academic career for idealistic, rather than pragmatic, reasons.

58. Considering the American cultural emphasis on greatness, it perhaps should come as no surprise that the genre of the tall tale has long struck a resonant chord in the American mind.

UNIT 4 인과 관계 구문

01 너무 ~해서 ~ 하다

- so + 형/부 + as to v : 너무 ~해서 v 하다
- not so 형/부 as to v : v할 정도로 ~하지는 않다

- so + 형/부 + that s v ~ : 너무 형/부 해서 S는 V하다
- not so + 형/부 + that s v ~ : S가 V할 정도로 ~하지는 않다

- so 형 + a(n) + 명 that s v ~ = such + a + 형 + 명 + that s v ~
  : 너무 형용사한 명사여서 S는 V하다

- such + that s v ~ = so great that s v ~
  : 너무 대단해서 s는 v하다

- too + 형/부 + to v ~ : 너무 ~해서 to v 할 수 없다

- not/never + 형/부 + to v
  : 아무리 ~해도 ~할 수 있다 / ~할 수 없을정도로 ~하지는 않다

- only too + 형/부 + to v : 너무 ~해서 ~하다

02 결과의 to v

- only to v : 오직 ~하기 위해서/그러나 v하다.
  ex) I studied really hard only to fail the exam.
  (나는 공부를 정말 열심히 했지만 시험에는 실패했다.)

- never to v : 그러나 v하지 못하다

문제풀이 기출문장을 통한 확인

59. What the psychologists discovered was that most of the people moved far enough away from the post so that tossing the rings around it was challenging but not so difficult as to be totally frustrating.

60. You may think that moving a short distance is so easy that you can do it in no time with little effort.

61. The sense of sight is so highly developed in humans that messages received from other senses are often ignored if they conflict with what is seen.

문제풀이 기출문장을 통한 확인

62. Public concern is so great in some countries that food companies are ending the use of GM crops altogether.

63. Afterimages can produce simultaneous contrast effects. If these are illusory colors, they nonetheless do much of the work of real colors, so much so that one can set up situations in which afterimage colors will be taken to be the colors of particular physical objects or of the light that illuminates them.

64. Teenagers' behavior changes when they realize others are too busy with their own lives to watch them.

문제풀이 기출문장을 통한 확인

65. People often sell old record albums, bottles, and books for pennies only to see them resold for tens or hundreds of dollars as parts of larger collections.

66. One of the forces that drive evolution is constant competition among species, in the course of which one species gains temporary advantages through an evolutionary innovation, only to be overtaken by a counter-innovation.

문제풀이 기출문장을 통한 확인

67. In much of social science, evidence is used only to affirm a particular theory — to search for the positive instances that uphold it.

68. Scientists have analyzed satellite images, never to give answers to what caused the eruption.

memo

UNIT 5 ~하자마자 구문

01 ~ 하자마자 구문

1. As soon as S + V ~, s v ~

= The moment s v ~ , s v ~

= On(upon) + n(-ing) ~, s v ~

= S no sooner V ~ than S V ~

= No sooner V S(의문문 어순 도치) ~ than S V ~

= S had hardly/scarcely p.p ~ when/before S V ~

= Hardly/Scarcely had S p.p ~ whan/before S V ~

문제풀이 기출문장을 통한 확인

69. Upon entering a record store, one encounters a wide variety of genres from easy listening to jazz and classical music.

70. Hardly had I come into contact with him when I determined to get to know him well. Never in my life have I been so strongly and immediately attracted to any man, before or since.

문제풀이 기출문장을 통한 확인

71. Health-conscious Americans increasingly find themselves confused by contradictory advice. No sooner do they learn the results of one study than they hear of one with opposite message.

72. As soon as you start to speak to someone else, your language serves as an instantly recognizable badge of your group identity.

memo

UNIT 6 부정 구문

01 부분 부정 : 모든게 다 그런 것은 아니다.

not + all (every, both, always, necessarily, completely)

02 이중 부정 : 강한 긍정

not, no 등의 부정어구 + 부정 의미의 단어(without 등)

주절 부정문 + 종속절 (명사절/형용사절/부사절) 부정문

03 can not (can't) ~ too

enough

over + 동사원형 : 아무리 ~해도 지나치지 않다.

It is impossible to over 동사원형

04 far from -ing/명사/형용사 : ~이기는커녕

be far from ~ : 절대 ~가 아니다.
(never)

05 by no means, not ~ by any means

= on no account, not ~ on any account

= in no way, not in any way : 결코 ~이 아닌

06 beyond + N : N를 할 수 없을정도로

07 have/has(be) + yet to v : 아직 ~하지 못했다.

문제풀이 기출문장을 통한 확인

73. Scientific and professional policy design does not necessarily escape the pitfalls of degenerative politics.

74. Not all children of successful people become successful themselves.

75. No matter how good your product is, remember that perfection of an existing product is not necessarily the best investment one can make.

문제풀이 기출문장을 통한 확인

76. Benjamin Bloom, an education psychologist, wrote in 1985 that none of his students achieved their goals without a supportive environment and a long and intensive period of training.

77. There is no basis for believing that technology will not cause new and unanticipated problems while solving the problems that it previously produced.

78. The black serpent, chaos, has a white dot in its head. The white serpent, order, has a black dot in its head. This is because chaos and order are interchangeable, as well as eternally juxtaposed. There is nothing so certain that it cannot vary.

문제풀이 기출문장을 통한 확인

79. We must remember that art is not necessarily beauty: that cannot be said too often.

80. It cannot be too often repeated that it is not helps but obstacles, not facilities but difficulties that make men great.

81. The only thing in the world which one can never receive or give too much is love. One does not spoil children by giving too much, but by giving them too little.

문제풀이 기출문장을 통한 확인

82. One of the commodities in life that most people can't get enough of is compliments.

83. Many people believe that it is critical to share similar, if not identical, beliefs and values with someone with whom they have a relationship. While this may seem preferable, it is far from mandatory.

84. Health is perhaps the most striking example of the paradoxical combination of smart elements and often-stupid results. We now benefit from vastly more access to information on diseases, diagnoses, and treatments on the Internet. But this is far from a golden age of healthy activity or intelligence about health.

문제풀이 기출문장을 통한 확인

85. As a matter of fact, the sense of sin, so far from being a cause of good life, is quite the reverse. It makes a man unhappy and it makes him feel inferior.

86. My 19-year-old son fell asleep driving to work this morning. He's lucky to be alive since his car was damaged beyond repair.

87. Distance learning has recently become prominent in the field of further education. However, much about the processes and the participants involved is yet to be fully understood.

memo

UNIT 7 목적 구문

01 ~ 하기 위해서

1. so as to v

= in order to v ~

= so that s v ~

= in order that s v ~

= with a view to n/ing ~

= for the purpose of ~

02 ~하지 않도록(않기 위해서)

2. lest S + (should) + V ~

= for fear (that) s (should) v ~

= so that s not v ~

= so as not to v, in order not to v

문제풀이 기출문장을 통한 확인

88. It is therefore important, if not essential, to maintain a clear focus in undertaking advocacy or mediation in order to ensure that the roles do not become blurred and therefore potentially counterproductive.

89. It was, therefore, important for the viewer to create a distance from the actions on the stage so as to facilitate interpretation of the content.

90. I have been working hard so that my family can enjoy an easy and convenient life.

문제풀이 기출문장을 통한 확인

91. When you travel, be sure to make your budget realistic in order that you can be confident that you will be able to pay for all aspects of the trip.

92. Some students with disease were found to have been hiding their infection and attended class for days for fear that they should ruin their school grades.

93. Furthermore, news-based tasks can be used as a context for students to demonstrate their knowledge with a view to identifying gaps in their understanding or weaknesses in their ability to make links between related areas of learning.

memo

UNIT 8 가정법 구문

가정법의 가장 중요한 원칙 : 가정법은 반대로 뒤집어서 보는 것이 핵심!
ex) If I were a bird, I would fly away(내가 새라면, 날아갈텐데)
→ 이 말의 뜻은 나는 내가 아니어서 날아갈 수 없다. 라고 받아들이는 훈련을 할 것!

01 가정법 과거 : 현재 사실의 반대

If S + 과거동사 ~, S + would/could/should/might + 동사 원형

* be 동사는 were로 쓴다.

02 가정법 과거 완료 : 과거 사실의 반대

If + S + had p.p ~, S + would/should/could/might + have p.p ~

03 혼합 가정법

If + S + had p.p ~, S + would/should/could/might + 동사원형 + now/today 등등

If + S 과거동사 ~, S would/should/could/might have p.p ~

* (If절이 역사적 사실일 때) → 해석은 그냥 가정법 과거 완료처럼 한다!

04 가정법 특수 표현

1. ~가 없다면/없었다면

① ~가 없다면 : If it were not for ~/were it not for/without/but for

② ~가 없었다면 : If it had not been for ~/had it not been for/
without/but for

2. 혹시라도 S가 V한다면

① If S + should V원 ~ , S V(주절의 동사엔 아무거나 올 수 있다.)
(과거, 과거완료, 현재완료 제외)
명령문

② If S + were to v ~ , S would/should/could/might 동사원형

05 I wish(if only), as if 가정법

1. I wish 가정법(~라면 좋을텐데)

- I wish that S + 과거동사 ~ : ~라면 좋을텐데
- I wish that S + had p.p ~ : ~였다면 좋을텐데

* I wish that 대신 if only로 써도 된다.

2. as if 가정법과 as if 단순 비유

- S V ~ as if S + 과거동사 : 마치 ~처럼
  (그렇지 않은데 그런 것처럼 이라는 의미)
- S V ~ as if S + had p.p : 마치 ~였던 것처럼
  (그런 적이 없었는데 그랬던 것처럼 이라는 의미)
- S V ~ as if S 현재동사 ~ : 마치 ~인 것처럼 (단순 비유)

06 가정법 도치

도치하는 방법

① If절의 If를 지운다.

② If절을 의문문의 어순으로 도치해준다.

* 단, 가정법 과거에서 If절의 동사가 일반동사일 때는 도치 불가능

문제풀이 기출문장을 통한 확인

94. If you knew me well, you would know that I am shameless enough to take all compliments at their face value and not to think that they might be mere flattery.

95. If I had told you the truth, you might have panicked and none of us would have made it.

96. The domestic oil, natural gas, or steel industry may require protection due to its importance to national defense. If it were not for protection, such industries might be weakened by foreign competition.

문제풀이 기출문장을 통한 확인

97. For instance, social order is maintained only on the condition that people repress their aggressive instincts and tendencies. However, for Freud, this repression takes an intolerably heavy toll on human psychology. Humans would not be able to handle this repression of their instincts were it not for some sort of psychological compensation to relieve the pressure.

98. If chaos that makes everything uncertain should distract our society, a leader is expected to restore normality immediately.

99. It is vital that all students and staff know what to do should we face a wildfire.

문제풀이 기출문장을 통한 확인

100. A quicksand may look like normal sand, but were you to step on it, the pressure from your foot would cause the sand to act more like a liquid and you'd sink right in.

101. We tend to take pride in our rationality and feel a bit ashamed of our emotions, as if rationality were more likely to be right and the emotions commensurately apt to be wrong.
rationality were more likely to be right and the emotions commensurately apt to be wrong.

102. We value sight above all things, and fortunate indeed should we be could we exchange our imperfect vision for sight like that of an eagle!

UNIT 9 It ~ that 강조 구문

01 It ~ that 강조와 가주어 진주어의 차이

- It is 명 that v ~ : It that 강조

- It is 명 that s vt O(x) : It that 강조

- It is 명 that s v ~(완전한 문장) : 가주어/진주어

- It is 형용사 that s v ~(완전한 문장) : 가주어/진주어

- It is 부사/부사구/부사절 that s v ~(완전한 문장) : It that 강조

* It that 강조일 때는 바로 It과 that을 지우고 생각해볼 것!

02 It is p.p that s v의 해석법

- It is를 people로 보고 p.p를 타동사로 보고
  that s v를 목적어처럼 보고 해석한다.

- It is held that s v : 사람들은 ~라고 주장한다/생각한다

03 가정법 특수 표현

- It is likely that s v ~ : S가 V할 가능성이 있다 (그렇게 될 것이다 라는 의미)

- It is more likely that s v : S가 V할 가능성이 높다 (그렇게 될 것이다 라는 의미)

- It is less likely that s v ~ : S가 V할 가능성이 낮다
  (그렇게 되지 않을 것이다 라는 의미)

- It is unlikely that s v ~ : S가 V할 가능성이 없다
  (그렇게 되지 않을 것이다 라는 의미)

- It follows that s v ~ : S가 V하는 것은 당연하다
  (이건 당연한 얘기이고 다음 문장이 주제문일 확률이 높다.)
  = It stands to reason that s v ~

- It does not follow that s v ~ : 반드시 S가 V한 것은 아니다 (부분부정)

- It seems that s v ~ : S가 V인 것처럼 보인다
  (appears)

- It happens that s v ~ : 우연히/공교롭게도 S는 V하다

- It turns out (proves) that s v ~ : S가 V임이 입증되다

- It occurs that s v ~ : S가 V하다는 생각이 떠오르다
  = It strikes O that s v ~ : O에게 S가 V하다는 생각이 떠오르다

- It used to be that s v ~ : S는 V 하곤 했다/S는 V였었다

- It might/may be that s v ~ : S는 V일지도 모른다

- It could/can be that s v ~ : S는 V일 것이다

문제풀이 기출문장을 통한 확인

103. It is often thinking of so many things and consideration of so many doubts that result in the difficulty to reach and act on a simple decision.

104. It is only when we let our minds wander that we make unexpected connections between things that we did not realize were connected. This can help you solve problems that previously seemed to be unsolvable.

105. It is believed that brightness of the Sun can be predicted theoretically.

문제풀이 기출문장을 통한 확인

106. This kind of decision making is the result of an authentic question generated by the learner on the basis of a genuine need to know and is one that inevitably requires more complex thinking. It is the search for meaning that organizes actor-centered questions and encourages the use of higher-order functions.

107. It is not just the newness of contemporary literature that makes it different, but also the context in which it is written and received, something which gives it a very interesting edge over the literature of the past.

문제풀이 기출문장을 통한 확인

108. It is likely that some children and young people have no idea of what needs to be changed in their life. The concept of having power and control over our lives to effect change is a fairly abstract one, and goal setting is not something we typically encourage young people to do, aside from reaching academic goals or passing exams.

109. It turns out that it's the sense of control that matters, even more so than what you actually do. If you have confidence that you can impact a situation, it will be less stressful. In contrast, a low sense of control may very well be the most stressful thing in the universe.

110. It follows that the most common alternative names for digital code and hypertext are multimedia, interactive media and digital media.

문제풀이 기출문장을 통한 확인

111. Sometimes, it seems that people simply like to try new things — they are interested in variety seeking, in which the priority is to vary one's product experiences, perhaps as a form of stimulation or to avoid being bored.

112. It appears that measures that protect drivers from the consequences of bad driving encourage bad driving.

113. It used to be that a photographer would look and then shoot, taking time to compose the image and look for important relationships within the scene before tripping the shutter, even if it was as rapid-fire as street photography.

UNIT 10 특이한 구문

01

have no choice but to v
option
alternative → ~할 수 밖에 없다

02

nothing but → 오로지(only)
anything but → never(절대 ~가 아니다)

03

take O for granted → O를 당연하게 여기다
take it for granted to v / that s v ~ : ~하는 것을 당연하게 여기다

04

The chances are that s v ~ : S가 V할 가능성이 있다
= Estimates are that s v ~ : 추정컨대 S는 V하다

05

It takes + 사람 + 시간 + to v ~ : to v = It takes + 시간 + for 명사 + to v ~
: to v하는 것은 (사람)에게 (~의) 시간이 들게 하다

It takes O to v ~: to v하는 것은 ~의 시간이 걸리다

* 시간의 목적어 자리엔 시간 명사 대신 long, short를 쓸 수도 있다.
long은 긴 시간, short는 짧은 시간 이라고 해석하면 된다.

문제풀이 기출문장을 통한 확인

114. Most organic farmers have no choice but to rely on chemicals as necessary supplements to their operations.

115. Uneducated people who could not read the book that was a dead language to them, saw nothing but all manner of pretty pictures in it.

116. The traditional Chinese manner of producing tea was anything but industrial and had remained unchanged for hundreds of years.

문제풀이 기출문장을 통한 확인

117. At times, coaches are so focused on helping athletes improve that they take good performance efforts for granted.

118. We take it for granted that people of different ages behave differently.

119. Chances are everything in the store from the layout and lighting to the music and even the smells has been organized to help shape your shopping experience — and to open your wallet.

문제풀이 기출문장을 통한 확인

120. Estimates are that 90 percent of the world's data has been created in the last five years. We're all drowning in information, a reality that makes even the simplest decisions — where to eat, which health plan to sign up for, which coffee maker to buy — more complicated.

121. "Once you've started, it can take just six weeks to see an improvement of up to 20 percent in your muscle capabilities," says Dr. Ward.

memo

정답과 해설

Part 1 문제 해설

Unit 1 1형식 P.12

1. The environmental adversities / actually contribute / to their longevity.

직독직해 해석

환경적인 역경들은 / 실제로 기여한다 / 그들의 장수에.

의역 해석

환경적인 역경들은 그들의 장수에 실제로 기여한다.

2. The new information / can contribute / to a completely different perspective / in finding / a solution, / thus producing / the Aha! Experience.

직독직해 해석

새로운 정보는 / 기여할 수 있다 / 완전히 다른 관점에 / 발견할 때 / 해결책을 / 따라서 생산한다 / 아하! 경험을

의역 해석

새로운 정보는 해결책을 발견할 때 완전히 다른 관점에 기여할 수 있고, 따라서 아하! 경험을 생산한다.

3. When the habitat / disappears, / a vast number of species / disappear / as well.

직독직해 해석

서식지가 / 사라질 때 / 수많은 종들은 / 사라진다 / 또한.

의역 해석

서식지가 사라지면 수많은 종들 또한 사라진다.

4. Growth / is always at the edges, / just outside the boundaries / of where you are / right now.

직독직해 해석

성장은 / 항상 가장자리에 있다 / 딱 경계선 밖에 / 너가 있는 장소의 / 현재.

의역 해석

성장은 항상 가장자리에, 즉 너가 현재 있는 장소의 딱 경계선 밖에 있다.

5. Often, / however, / regulations / on meeting / reporting requirements / do not work / adequately, / as the Enron scandal / in 2001 / clearly illustrates.

직독직해 해석

종종, / 그러나, / 규칙들은 / 충족시키는 것에 대한 / 보고 필요조건들을 / 작동하지 않는다 / 적절하게 / 엔론 스캔들이 / 2001년에 / 명백하게 보여주듯이.

의역 해석

그러나, 2001년 엔론 스캔들이 명백하게 보여주듯이, 종종 보고 필요조건들을 충족시키는 것에 관한 규칙들은 적절하게 작동하지 않는다.

6. There were / no vocalizations / that I was aware of / that might indicate / Sarah / was distressed / by Harper's thievery, / nor that Sheba / was trying / to appease / any distress.

직독직해 해석

어떠한 목소리들도 없었다 / 내가 알고 있던 / 나타내줄지도 모르는 / 사라가 / 고통스러워 했다는 것을 / Harper의 도둑질 때문에, / 그리고 (목소리들도 없었다) Sheba(매력적인 미녀)가 / 노력하고 있었다는 / 달래기 위해 / 어떤 고통이든

의역 해석

내가 알고 있던 것들 중에 사라가 Harper의 도둑질 때문에 고통스러워하고 있다는 것을 나타내줄지도 모르는 어떤 목소리들도 없었고, 그녀가 어떤 고통이든 달래기 위해 노력하고 있었다는 어떠한 목소리들도 없었다.

7. Scientific and professional expertise / often relies / on a particular type of knowledge / which is limited / to utility and rationality considerations.

직독직해 해석

과학적이고 전문적인 지식은 / 종종 의존한다 / 특정한 종류의 지식에 / 제한된 / 유용성과 이성적인 고려사항들에

의역 해석

과학적이고 전문적인 지식은 종종 유용성과 이성적인 고려사항들에 제한된 특정한 종류의 지식에 의존한다.

8. The Health Management Program / lasts / for six weeks / and consists / of three different components: / Daily Targets, Walking Plans, and Eating Plans.

직독직해 해석

건강 관리 프로그램은 / 지속된다 / 6주 동안 / 그리고 구성된다 / 세 가지의 다양한 구성요소들로: / 데일리 타겟, 걷기 계획, 그리고 먹기 계획으로.

의역 해석

건강 관리 프로그램은 6주 동안 지속되고 3가지의 다양한 구성요소들로 구성된다: 매일 목표, 걷기 계획, 먹기 계획

9. When there is / a discrepancy / between the verbal message and the nonverbal message, / the latter / typically weighs / more / in forming / a judgment.

직독직해 해석

있을 때 / 차이가 / 언어적인 메시지와 비언어적인 메시지 사이에, / 후자는 / 보통 작용한다 / 더 / 형성하는데 있어서 / 판단을

의역 해석

언어적인 메시지와 비언어적인 메시지 사이에 차이가 있을 때, 후자는 판단을 형성하는데 있어서 보통 더 작용한다.

10. The train / arrived / at my destination / ten minutes early, / which was perfect, / as I / was due / to present / my new idea / to the company / at 10 a.m.

직독직해 해석

기차는 / 도착했다 / 내 목적지에 / 10분 일찍, / 그리고 그것은 완벽했다, / 나는 / 예정이었기 때문에 / 제공할 / 내 새로운 아이디어를 / 회사에 / 오전 10시에.

의역 해석

기차는 목적지에 10분 일찍 도착했고 그것은 정말 완벽했다. 왜냐하면 난 오전 10시에 회사에 새로운 아이디어를 제공할 예정이었기 때문이다.

Unit 2 2형식 P.18

11. An old teapot / which has lost / its lid / becomes an ideal container / for a bunch of roses / picked / from the garden.

직독직해 해석

오래된 주전자는 / 잃어버린 / 뚜껑을 / 이상적인 용기가 된다 / 한다발의 장미를 위한 / 꺾여진 / 정원으로부터.

의역 해석

뚜껑을 잃어버린 오래된 주전자는 정원으로부터 꺾인 한 다발의 장미를 위한 이상적인 용기가 되어준다.

12. A tool / may be awkward / to use / and inefficient, / or possibly even dangerous/ —a hammer / is a good example. / However, / it / may be so familiar / to so many people / that they / have become accustomed / to its disadvantages / and may be able to use / it / very effectively, / despite the disadvantages and inconvenience.

직독직해 해석

도구는 / 어색할지도 모른다. / 사용하기에 / 그리고 비효율적일지도 모른다, / 또는 아마 심지어 위험하다 / 즉, 망치는 / 좋은 예시이다. / 그러나, / 이것은 / 너무 친숙해졌을지도 모른다 / 매우 많은 사람들에게 / 그래서 그들이 / 익숙해졌다 / 이것의 단점들에 / 그리고 사용할 수 있을지도 모른다 / 이것을 / 매우 효과적으로, / 단점과 불편에도 불구하고.

의역 해석

도구는 사용하기가 어색할지도 모르고 비효율적이며, 심지어는 위험할지도 모른다. 그 가장 좋은 예시가 망치이다. 그런데, 이것이 매우 많은 사람들에게 너무 친숙해져서 단점들과 불편한 것에도 불구하고 이것을 매우 효과적으로 사용할 수 있을지도 모른다.

13. Small changes / in the sensory properties / of foods / are sufficient / to increase / food intake.

직독직해 해석

작은 변화들은 / 감각적인 특성들에 대한 / 음식의 / 충분하다 / 증가시키기에 / 음식 섭취를.

의역 해석

음식의 감각적인 특성들에 대한 작은 변화들은 음식 섭취를 증가시키기에 충분하다.

14. These / are among the basic questions / that were addressed / at the first world meeting / on the environment, / attended / by more than 100 world leaders and 30,000 other scientists, newspeople, and citizens concerned.

직독직해 해석

이러한 것들은 / 기본적인 질문들 중에 있다 / 다뤄졌던 / 세계 첫 번째 회의에서 / 환경에 대한, / 참석되어진 / 100명 이상의 세계 리더와 30,000명의 다른 과학자, 신문기자, 그리고 관련 시민들에 의해

의역 해석

이러한 것들은 환경에 대한 세계 첫 번째 회의에서 다뤄졌던 기본적인 질문들 중에 있다. 그리고 그 회의는 100명 이상의 세계 리더와 30,000명의 다른 과학자, 신문지가, 그리고 관련 시민들에 의해 참석되어졌다.

15. Comparison / with the inferior / is self-enhancement / at work. / But what / happens / when the only available comparison target / we / have / is superior / or better off / than we are?

직독직해 해석

비교는 / 더 열등한 사람들과의 / 자기 강화이다 / 일에서. / 그런데 무엇이 / 발생하는가 / 유일하게 이용가능한 비교 타겟이 / 우리가 / 가지고 있는 / 더 우수하거나 / 더 부유하다면 / 우리보다.

의역 해석

더 열등한 사람들과의 비교는 일에서 자기 강화요소이다. 그런데 우리가 가지고 있는 유일하게 비교가 가능한 대상들이 우리보다 더 부유하거나 우수하다면 무엇이 발생하는가?

16. Hence, / raising / awareness / of children / from a very early age / about the particular characteristics / of SNS / and the potential long-term impact / of a seemingly trivial act / is crucial.

직독직해 해석

따라서, / 기르는 것은 / 인식을 / 아이들의 / 매우 어릴때부터 / 특별한 특징들에 대한 / sns의 / 그리고 잠재적인 장기 영향에 대한 / 언뜻 보기엔 사소한 활동의 / 중요하다.

의역 해석

따라서, 매우 어릴 때부터 sns의 특별한 특징과 언뜻 보기엔 사소한 이 활동의 잠재적인 장기 영향력에 대한 인식을 길러주는 것은 중요하다.

17. Disease, / as a sanction / against social misbehavior, / becomes one of the most important pillars / of order / in such societies.

직독직해 해석

질병은, / 벌칙으로서 / 사회적인 잘못된 행동에 대한 / 가장 중요한 특징들 중의 하나가 된다 / 질서의 / 그러한 사회에서.

의역 해석

사회적인 잘못된 행동에 대한 벌칙으로서 질병은 그러한 사회에서 질서의 가장 중요한 특징들 중의 하나가 된다.

18. Natural preference / for foods / appears to be specific evolved mechanisms, / designed / to deal with / the adaptive problem / of food selection, / and coordinate consumption patterns / with physical needs.

직독직해 해석

타고난 선호도는 / 음식에 대한 / 특별하게 진화된 기제인 것처럼 보인다. / 설계되어진 / 해결하기 위해서 / 적응의 문제를 / 음식 선택의 / 그리고 맞추기 위해서 / 소비 패턴을 / 신체적인 욕구들과.

의역 해석

음식에 대한 타고난 선호도는 음식 선택에 대한 적응의 문제를 해결하고 소비 패턴을 신체적인 욕구들과 맞추기 위해서 설계되어진 특별하게 진화된 기제인 것처럼 보인다.

19. Indeed, / print-oriented novelists / seem doomed / to disappear, / as electronic media and computer games / are becoming more influential.

직독직해 해석

사실, / 인쇄 중심의 소설가들은 / 운명인 것처럼 보인다 / 사라질 / 전자 매체와 컴퓨터 게임들이 / 더 영향력을 행사하면서.

의역 해석

사실, 전자 매체와 컴퓨터 게임들이 더 영향력을 행사하면서 인쇄 중심의 소설가들은 사라질 운명인 것처럼 보인다.

20. Falling in love / is like being wrapped / in a magical cloud. / The air / feels fresher, / the flowers / smell sweeter, / food / tastes more delicious, / and the stars / shine / more brilliantly / in the night sky.

직독직해 해석

사랑에 빠지는 것은 / 쌓이는 것과 같다 / 마법의 구름에. / 공기는 / 더 신선하게 느껴지고, / 꽃은 / 더 달콤하게 냄새가 나고, / 음식은 / 더 맛있게 느껴지고, / 그리고 별들은 / 빛난다 / 더 밝게 / 밤하늘에서.

의역 해석

사랑에 빠진다는 것은 마법의 구름에 휩싸이는 것과 같다. 공기는 더 신선하고, 꽃은 더 달콤한 냄새가 나고, 음식은 더 맛있어지고, 별들은 밤하늘에서 더 밝게 빛난다.

21. You / look at / the trees and the mountains / through windows / that are wet / with rain / from a storm, / and everything / looks shapeless and out of focus.

직독직해 해석

당신은 / 본다 / 나무와 산을 / 창문을 통해 / 젖은 / 비로 / 폭풍으로부터의 / 그리고 모든 것들은 / 형체가 없어보이고 초점이 없어 보인다.

의역 해석

당신은 나무와 산을 폭풍으로부터의 비로 젖은 창문을 통해 본다. 그리고 모든 것들은 형체가 없어보이고 초점이 없어 보인다.

22. So the only thing / you / can do / is try / to fail / faster / so that you / can move / onto the next idea.

직독직해 해석

그래서 유일한 것은 / 당신이 / 할 수 있는 / 노력하는 것이다 / 실패하기 위해서 / 더 빠르게 / 당신이 / 움직일 수 있도록 / 다음 아이디어로.

의역 해석

그래서 당신이 할 수 있는 유일한 것은 당신이 더 빠르게 다음 아이디어로 움직일 수 있도록 더 빠르게 실패하기 위해 노력하는 것이다.

23. The good news / is that it's never too late / to start / building up / muscle strength, / regardless of your age. / Ideally, / though, / it's best / to start / in your mid-forties / when muscle mass / starts / to decline significantly.

직독직해 해석

좋은 뉴스는 / 아무리 늦어도 / 시작할 수 있다는 것이다 / 강화하는 것을 / 근육의 힘을 / 당신의 나이에 관계없이. / 이상적으로, / 그러나, / 최고다 / 시작하는 것이 / 당신의 40대 중반에 / 근육 덩어리가 / 시작하는 / 심각하게 감소하는 것을.

의역 해석

좋은 소식은 나이에 관계없이 아무리 늦어도 근육의 힘을 강화하는 것을 시작할 수 있다는 것이다. 그러나 이상적으로는 근육 덩어리가 현저하게 감소하기 시작하는 40대 중반에 시작하는 것이 가장 좋다.

24. It / is easy / to find / examples / of correlations / which are far more systematic / than could occur / by chance / and yet / which it would be absurd / to treat / as evidence / of a direct causal link.

직독직해 해석

쉽다 / 발견하는 것은 / 예시의 / 연관관계의 / 훨씬 더 체계적인 / 발생할 수 있는 것 보다 / 우연히 / 그러나 / 터무니없는 / 다루는 것이 / 증거로서 / 직접적인 인과관계의.

의역 해석

우연히 발생할 수 있는 것보단 훨씬 더 체계적이지만 직접적인 인과관계의 증거로서 다루는 것은 터무니 없는 연관관계의 예시들을 발견하는 것은 쉽다.

25. Parental enthusiasm / for head-up motor accomplishments / from their infants / is not at all misplaced, / for they / are, indeed, milestones of development.misplaced, / for they / are, indeed, milestones of development.

직독직해 해석

부모의 열정은 / 머리를 드는 행동을 성취하는 것에 대한 / 그들의 아이로부터 / 전혀 잘못되지 않았다 / 왜냐하면 그것들은 / 실제로 개발의 중요한 단계이기 때문이다.

의역 해석

그들의 아이가 머리를 드는 행동을 성취하는 것에 대한 부모의 열정은 결코 잘못되지 않았다. 왜냐하면 그것들은 실제로 개발의 중요한 단계이기 때문이다.

26. Politics / cannot be suppressed, / whichever policy process / is employed / and however sensitive and respectful / of differences / it might be. / In other words, / there is no end / to politics. / It is wrong / to think / that proper institutions, knowledge, methods of consultation, or participatory mechanisms / can make / disagreement / go away.

직독직해 해석

정치는 / 억압될 수 없다 / 어떤 정책 과정이 / 이용 되든지 간에 / 그리고 얼마나 예민하고 존중해주든지간에 / 차이점에 대해 / 이것(정치)이. / 다시 말해서 / 끝이 없다 / 정치에는. / 잘못이다 / 생각하는 것은 / 적절한 제도, 지식, 상담 방법, 또는 참여 방식들이 / 만들 수 있다고 / 의견 불일치가 / 사라지게.

의역 해석

어떤 정책 과정이 이용되든지, 그리고 이 정치가 차이점에 대해 얼마나 민감하고 존중해주든지간에 정치는 억압될 수 없다. 다시 말해서 정치에는 끝이 없다. 적절한 제도, 지식, 상담 방법, 또는 참여 방식들이 의견불일치를 사라지게 만들 수 있다고 생각하는 것은 잘못이다.

27. One of my dreams / was to become a photographer. / That dream / came to an abrupt halt / in a photography class. / There was / no denying / in the other students' pictures / that they / were far more talented / than I was.

직독직해 해석

제 꿈들 중 한 가지는 / 사진사가 되는 것이었습니다. / 그 꿈은 / 갑작스레 멈추게 되었습니다 / 사진 교실에서. / 부정할 수 없었습니다 / 다른 학생들의 사진에서 / 그들이 훨씬 더 재능이 있다는 것을 / 저보다.

의역 해석

제 꿈들 중 한 가지는 사진사가 되는 것이었습니다. 그 꿈은 사진 교실에서 갑자기 중단하게 되었습니다. 다른 학생들의 그림에서 저보다 그들이 훨씬 더 재능이 있다는 것을 부정할 수 없었습니다.

28. People / are much more concerned / about catching / the ball / than throwing / it. What this / demonstrates / is that it's equally as important / to the success / of the exercise / that the person / you're / throwing to / catches / the ball / as that you are able to catch / the ball.

직독직해 해석

사람들은 / 훨씬 더 걱정합니다 / 잡는 것에 대해서 / 공을 / 던지는 것 보다 / 그것을. / 이것이 / 입증해주는 것은 / 동등하게 중요하다는 것입니다 / 성공에 / 활동의 / 사람이 / 당신이 던지는 / 잡는 것이 / 공을 / 당신이 / 잡을 수 있는 것 만큼이나 / 공을.

의역 해석

사람들은 공을 던지는 것보다 공을 잡는 것에 대해서 훨씬 더 걱정합니다. 이것이 입증해주는 것은 당신이 공을 잡을 수 있는 것 만큼이다 당신이 공을 던지고 있는 상대가 공을 잡는 것이 이 운동의 성공에 동등하게 중요하다는 것입니다.

29. The essential argument / here / is that the capitalist mode / of production / is affecting / peasant production / in the less developed world / in such a way / as to limit / the production / of staple foods, / thus causing / a food problem.

직독직해 해석

필수적인 주장은 / 여기에서 / 자본주의적인 방식이 / 생산의 / 영향을 주고 있다는 것이다 / 농부들의 생산에 / 덜 발달한 국가에서 / 같은 방식으로 / 제한하는 것과 / 생산을 / 주식의, / 따라서 야기한다 / 음식 문제를.

의역 해석

여기에서의 필수적인 주장은 자본주의적인 생산 방식이 덜 발달한 국가에서 주식의 생산을 제한해서 음식 문제를 야기하는 것과 같은 방식으로 농부들의 생산에 영향을 주고 있다는 것이다.

Unit 3 3형식 P.30

30. Subscriptions / account for / almost 90 percent / of total magazine circulation. Single-copy, or newsstand sales / account for / the rest.

직독직해 해석

정기구독은 / 차지한다 / 거의 90퍼센트를 / 전체 잡지 판매의. 단행본, 혹은 뉴스 가판대 판매가 / 차지한다 / 나머지를

의역 해석

정기 구독이 전체 잡지 판매의 90퍼센트를 차지한다. 단행본, 가판대, 그리고 판매가 나머지를 차지한다.

31. One / wonders / whether our children's inherent capacity / to recognize, / classify, / and order / information / about their environment / — abilities / once essential / to our very survival / — is slowly evolving / to facilitate / life / in their increasingly virtualized world.

직독직해 해석

사람은 / 궁금해한다 / 자신의 아이들의 타고난 능력이 / 인식하고, / 분류하고 / 정리하는 / 정보를 / 그들의 환경에 대해서 / 즉 능력이 / 한 때 필수적이었던 / 우리의 바로 그 생존에 / 느리게 발전하는지 아닌지를 / 용이하게 하기 위해서 / 삶을 / 그들의 점점 더 가상화되는 세상에서.

의역 해석

사람은 자신의 아이들이 우리의 생존에 한 때 필수적이었던 능력인 그들의 환경에 대한 정보를 인식하고 분류하고 정리하는 아이들의 타고난 능력이 그들의 점점 더 강상화된 세상에서 삶을 용이하기 위해서 느리게 발전하는지 아닌지를 궁금해한다.

32. One / may wonder / if literary fiction / is destined / to become an old-fashioned genre / to be preserved / in a museum / like an extinct species.

직독직해 해석

사람은 / 궁금해할지도 모른다 / 그들의 문학 소설이 / 운명인지 아닌지를 / 구식의 장르가 될 / 보존될 / 박물관에서 / 멸종된 종들처럼.

의역 해석

사람은 그들의 문학 소설이 멸종된 종들처럼 박물관에 보존되는 구식의 장르가 될 운명인지 아닌지를 궁금해할지도 모른다.

33. Geniuses / don't necessarily have / a higher success rate / than other creators; / they / simply do more / — and they / do / a range of different things.

직독직해 해석

천재들은 / 반드시 가지고 있는 것은 아니다 / 더 높은 성공률을 / 다른 창조자들보다; / 그들은 단순히 더 많은 것을 한다 / 그리고 그들은 / 한다 / 다양한 것들을.

의역 해석

천재들은 반드시 다른 창조자들보다 더 높은 성공률을 가지고 있는 것은 아니다. 그들은 단순히 더 많은 것들을 하고 다양한 것들을 한다.

34. We / could have seen / something / many times before, / but / as the result of having / new skills or competence, / we / discover / new or different aspects / of that object.

직독직해 해석

우리는 / 봤을 것이다 / 어떤 것을 / 많이 이전에, / 그런데 / 가지는 것의 결과로서 / 새로운 기술이나 능력을 / 우리는 / 발견한다 / 새롭거나 다른 측면들을 / 그 물체의

의역 해석

우리는 어떤 것을 예전에 많이 봤을 것이다. 그런데 새로운 능력이나 기술을 가지는 것의 결과로서 우리는 그 물체의 새롭거나 다른 측면들을 발견한다.

35. I / have had / the opportunity / to look over / your poems, / and I / feel / that they / show / considerable promise, / despite your youth and lack of experience in this genre.

직독직해 해석

저는 / 가져왔습니다 / 기회를 / 검토할 / 당신의 시를, / 그리고 전 / 느낍니다 / 그것들이 / 보여준다는 것을 / 상당한 가능성을, / 당신의 젊음과 이 분야에서의 경험 부족에도 불구하고

의역 해석

저는 당신의 시를 검토할 기회를 가져왔고, 전 당신의 젊음과 이 분야에서의 경험 부족에도 불구하고 그 시들이 상당한 가능성을 보여준다고 느낍니다.

36. Industries / are competitively changing / their businesses / into e-businesses, / and thus the demand / for the required workforce / is expected / to grow.

직독직해 해석

산업들은 / 경쟁적으로 바꾸고 있다 / 그들의 산업을 / e-비즈니스로, / 따라서 수요는 / 필요로 되어지는 노동력에 대한 / 예상된다. / 성장할 것으로.

의역 해석

산업들은 경쟁적으로 자신들의 산업을 e-산업으로 바꾸고 있다. 따라서 필요한 노동력에 대한 수요는 증가할 것으로 예상된다.

37. Finally, / local residents / may feel / that marketing process / reduces / their identities / to mere commercial transactions, / and they / may believe / they / sacrifice what is unique and special / about their place.

직독직해 해석

마침내, / 지역 주민들은 / 느낄지도 모른다 / 마케팅 과정은 / 전락시킨다고 / 그들의 정체성을 / 단순한 상업적인 거래로, / 그리고 그들은 / 믿을지도 모른다 / 그들이 / 희생한다고 / 독특하고 특별한 것을 / 그들의 장소에 대한.

의역 해석

마침내, 지역 주민들은 마케팅 과정은 자신들의 정체성을 단순한 상업적인 거래로 전락시킨다고 느낄지도 모른다. 그리고 그들은 그들의 장소에 대한 독특하고 특별한 것을 희생한다고 믿을지도 모른다.

38. No matter how hard / you may try / to produce / an objective paper, / the fact / is that every choice / you / make / as you write / is influenced / to some extent / by your personal beliefs and opinions. / What you / tell / your readers / is truth, in other words, is influenced, / sometimes without your knowledge, / by a multitude of factors: / your environment, / upbringing, / and education; / your attitude / toward your audience; your career goals; and your ambitions / for the paper / you / are writing.

직독직해 해석

아무리 열심히 / 당신이 노력할지라도 / 만들기 위해 / 객관적인 보고서를, / 사실은 / 모든 선택이 / 당신이 / 하는 / 당신이 쓰면서 / 영향받는다는 것이다 / 어느정도는 / 당신의 개인적 믿음과 의견에. / 당신이 / 말하는 것은 / 당신의 독자들에게 / 사실이라고 / 다시말해서, / 영향 받는다, / 때때로 당신이 아는 것 없이(알아차리지 못하고, / 대다수의 요인에 의해 / 당신의 환경, / 양육, / 그리고 교육, / 당신의 태도 / 대중을 향한 / 당신의 커리어 목표 그리고 당신의 야망 / 보고서에 대한 / 당신이 쓰고 있는

의역 해석

당신이 아무리 열심히 객관적인 보고서를 만들어내기 위해 노력할지라도, 팩트는 당신이 무엇인가를 쓸 때 당신이 하는 모든 선택은 어느정도 개인적 믿음과 의견에 영향을 받는다는 것이다. 당신이 독자들에게 사실이라고 말하는 것은, 다시 말해서 때때로는 당신이 알아차리지도 못한채로 환경, 양육, 교육, 대중을 향한 당신의 태도, 커리어의 목표, 당신이 쓰고 있는 보고서에 대한 당신의 야망에 의해 영향을 받는다.

39. We've / emphasized / that hereditary factors / are critical / in determining / which children / can look forward / to being outstanding, and perhaps even elite, athletes. However, / the effects / of genetics / are never absolute / because genes / do not operate / in isolation. / We / cannot undervalue / the influence / of the environments / in which we / live /—natural, social, and athletic.

▮직독직해 해석

우리는 / 강조해왔다 / 유전적 요인들이 / 중요하다는 것을 / 결정할 때 / 어떤 아이들이 / 기대할 수 있는지 / 뛰어난, 아마도 엘리트 운동선수가 되는 것을. / 그런데, / 영향은 / 유전자의 / 절대 정확하지 않다 / 왜냐하면 유전자는 / 작동하지 않기 때문이다 / 혼자서는. / 우리는 / 과소평가할 수 없다 / 영향을 / 환경의 / 우리가 / 사는 / 자연적인, 사회적인, 그리고 운동의

▮의역 해석

우리는 어떤 아이들이 뛰어나고 엘리트 운동선수가 되는 것을 기대할 수 있는지를 결정할 때 유전적 요인들이 중요하다는 것을 강조해왔다. 그런데, 유전자는 혼자서 작동하는 것이 아니기 때문에 유전자의 영향은 절대 완전한 것이 아니다. 우리는 우리가 사는 자연적인, 사회적인, 운동의 환경의 영향을 무시할 수 없다.

40. People / who change / do not question / whether change / is possible / or look for / reasons / they / cannot change. / They / simply decide / on a change / they / want / and do / what is necessary / to accomplish / it.

▮직독직해 해석

사람들은 / 변하는 / 의문을 제기하지 않는다 / 변화가 / 가능한지 아닌지를 / 또는 찾지 않는다 / 이유를 / 그들이 / 바뀔 수 없는. / 그들은 / 단순히 결정한다 / 변화에 대해서 / 그들이 / 원하는 / 그리고 한다 / 필수적인 것을 / 성취하기 위해 / 이것을.

▮의역 해석

변화하는 사람들은 변화가 가능한지 아닌지에 대해 의문을 제기하지 않고 그들이 바뀔 수 없는 이유를 찾지 않는다. 그들은 단순히 그들이 원하는 변화에 대해 결정을 하고 이것을 성취하기 위해 필수적인 것을 한다.

41. Whether their grandchildren / have / special needs / or not, / grandparents / shouldn't overlook / the value / of incidental learning experiences.

▮직독직해 해석

그들의 손자들이 / 가지고 있든지 아니든지간에 / 특별한 욕구를, / 조부모님들은 / 간과해서는 안된다 / 가치를 / 우연한 배움의 경험의.

▮의역 해석

그들의 손자들이 특별한 욕구를 가지고 있든지 아니든지간에, 조부모님들은 우연한 배움 경험의 가치를 간과해서는 안된다.

42. 73 percent / of Canadian voters / surveyed / denied / in the strongest possible terms / that their votes / had been influenced / by physical appearance; / only 14 percent / even allowed for / the possibility / of such influence.

▮직독직해 해석

73퍼센트는 / 캐나다 투표자들의 / 조사된 / 부정했다 / 가능한 한 가장 강력한 어조로 / 그들의 투표가 / 영향 받았다는 것을 / 외모에 의해; / 오로지 14퍼센트만이 / 심지어 여지를 줬다 / 가능성을 / 그러한 영향력의.

▮의역 해석

조사된 캐나다 투표자들의 73퍼센트는 가능한 한 가장 강력한 어조로 그들의 투표가 외모에 의해 영향 받았다는 것을 부정했다. 그리고 오로지 14퍼센트만이 그러한 영향력의 가능성에 대해 여지를 줬다(어느정도는 인정을 했다.

43. Today the term artist / is used / to refer to / a broad range of creative individuals / across the globe / from both past and present.

직독직해 해석

오늘날 아티스트라는 용어는 / 사용된다 / 나타내기 위해서 / 다양한 창의적인 개인들을 / 전세계에 걸쳐 / 과거와 현재로부터 둘 다.

의역 해석

오늘날 아티스트라는 용어는 전세계에서 과거와 현재로부터 둘 다 다양한 창의적인 개인들을 나타내기 위해서 사용된다.

44. When deciding / whether to invest / in a company, / for example, / they / may take into account / the people / at the helm; / the current and potential size / of its market; / net profits; / and its past, present, and future stock value, / among other pieces of information.

직독직해 해석

결정할 때 / 투자해야할지 말아야할지 / 회사에, / 예를 들어, / 그들은 / 고려할지도 모른다 / 사람들을 / 책임지고 있는; / 현재와 잠재적인 크기를 / 이것의 시장의; / 순 수익을; / 그리고 이것의 과거, 현재, 그리고 미래 주식 가치를, / 다른 모든 종류의 정보 중에서.

의역 해석

예를 들어 회사에 투자해야할지 말아야할지를 결정할 때 그들은 다른 정보들 중에서 책임자들, 현재와 잠재적인 시장의 크기, 순 수익을, 그리고 이것의 과거, 현재, 그리고 미래 주식 가치를 고려할지도 모른다.

45. In addition to protecting / the rights / of authors / so as to encourage / the publication / of new creative works, / copyright / is also supposed to place / reasonable time limits / on those rights / so that outdated works / may be incorporated / into new creative efforts.

직독직해 해석

보호하는 것 이외에도 / 권리를 / 작가의 / 장려하기 위해서 / 출판을 / 새로운 창의적인 작품들의, / 저작권은 / 또한 둬야만 한다 / 합리적인 시간 제한을 / 그러한 권리들에 / 구식의 작품들이 / 통합될 수 있도록 / 새로운 창의적인 노력으로.

의역 해석

새로운 창의적인 작품의 출판을 장려하기 위해 작가의 권리를 보호하는 것 이외에도, 저작권은 구식의 작품들이 새로운 창의적인 노력으로 통합될 수 있도록 그러한 권리들에 합리적인 시간 제한도 둬야만 한다.

46. Supporters of Copyright Act / like / to defend / these increases / with tales / of starving writers and their impoverished descendants, / but in reality the beneficiaries / are more likely to be transnational publishing companies.

직독직해 해석

저작권 법의 지지자들은 / 좋아한다 / 옹호하기를 / 이 증가들을 / 이야기들을 지닌채로 / 굶주리는 작가들과 그들의 가난한 후손들에 대한, / 그러나 실제로 수혜자들은 / 초국가적 출판 회사일 가능성이 높다.

의역 해석

저작권 법을 지지하는 사람들은 굶주리는 작가들과 그들의 가난한 후손들에 대한 이야기를 들어서 이러한 증가들을 옹호하기를 좋아하지만, 실제로 수혜자들은 초국가적 대기업들일 가능성이 높다.

47. Society, / through ethical and economic constraints, / exerts / a powerful influence / on what science / accomplishes. / At the same time, / the results / of science / have / profound, and sometimes unexpected impacts / on every human being / on earth.

직독직해 해석

사회는, / 윤리적이고 경제적인 제한사항들을 통해 / 준다 / 강력한 영향을 / 과학이 / 성취하는 것에. / 동시에, / 결과는 / 과학의 / 준다 / 심오하고 때때로는 예상치 못한 영향을 / 모든 인간에 / 지구에 있는.

의역 해석

사회는 윤리적이고 경제적인 제한사항들을 통해 과학이 성취하는 것에 강력한 영향을 준다. 동시에 과학의 결과물들은 지구상에 있는 모든 인간들에게 심오하고 때때로는 예상치 못한 영향을 준다.

48. Researchers / have suggested / that maintaining / good social relations / depends / on two complementary processes: / being sensitive / to the needs / of others / and being motivated / to pay / compensation / when a violation / does occur. / In short, / maintaining / good social relations / depends / on the capacity for guilt.

직독직해 해석

연구자들은 / 제안해왔다 / 유지하는 것이 / 좋은 사회적 관계를 / 달려있다고 / 두 가지의 보충적인 과정들에 / 즉 민감해지는 것이다 / 욕구에 / 다른 사람들의 / 그리고 동기부여되는 것이다 / 지불하도록 / 보상을 / 위반이 / 발생했을 때. / 요컨대, / 유지하는 것이 / 좋은 사회적 관계를 / 달려있다 / 죄의식에.

의역 해석

연구자들은 좋은 사회적 관계를 유지하는 것이 두 가지 보충적인 과정들에 달려있다고 제안해왔다. 즉 첫 번째는 다른 사람들의 욕구에 민감해지는 것이고 무엇인가 위반이 발생했을 때 보상을 지불하도록 동기부여되는 것이다. 요컨대, 좋은 사회적인 관계를 유지하는 것은 죄의식을 느끼는 것에 달려있다.

49. Organizations / with job openings / are looking / to fill / a slot / in one area, / and they / need / someone / who can jump in / right away.

직독직해 해석

조직들은 / 공석을 지닌 / 원하고 있다 / 채우기를 / 빈자리를 / 한 영역에서, / 그리고 그들은 / 필요하다 / 누군가가 / 시작할 수 있는 / 당장.

의역 해석

공석이 있는 조직들은 한 영역에서 빈 자리를 채우기를 원하고 있고, 그들은 당장 시작할 수 있는 누군가가 필요하다.

50. The roadside / is crowded / with locals, / and their brains / are crowded / with local knowledge, / but we / are too arrogant and embarrassed / to ask / the way.

직독직해 해석

길가는 / 가득 차 있다 / 지역 주민들로, / 그리고 그들의 뇌는 / 가득찬다 / 지역의 지식들로, / 그러나 우리는 / 너무 거만하고 당황해서 / 물어볼 수 없었다 / 길을.

의역 해석

길가는 지역 주민들로 가득 차 있었고 그들의 머리 속엔 지역에 대한 지식들로 가득 차 있었다. 그러나 우리는 너무 거만하고 당황해서 길을 물어볼 수 없었다.

51. Bold claims / were made / by critics / of the day / who averred / that Russian technology / wasn't advanced / enough / to perform / an wonderful feat.

직독직해 해석

대담한 주장이 / 되어졌다 / 비평가들에 의해 / 그날의 / 단언했던 / 러시아의 기술이 / 발전하지 않았다고 / 충분히 / 수행할 정도로 / 놀라운 업적을.

의역 해석

러시아 기술이 놀라운 업적을 수행할 정도로 충분히 발전하지는 않았다고 단언했던 그날의 비평가들에 의해 대담한 주장이 제기되었다.

52. It's not so much that your memory / of last week's lunch / has disappeared; / if provided / with the right cue, / like where you / ate it, / or whom you / ate / it / with, / you / would likely recall / what had been on your plate. / Rather, / it's difficult / to remember / last week's lunch / because your brain / has filed / it / away / with all the other lunches / you've / ever eaten / as just another lunch.

직독직해 해석

당신의 기억이 / 지난주 점심에 대한 / 사라졌다기 보다는 / 만약 제공받는다면 / 올바른 신호를 / 어디에서 당신이 / 그것을 먹었는지처럼, / 혹은 누구와 당신이 / 먹었는지 / 그것을 / 함께 / 당신은 떠올릴 가능성이 있다 / 당신의 쟁반 위에 있었던 것을. / 오히려, / 어렵다 / 기억하는 것은 / 지난주의 점심을 / 왜냐하면 당신의 뇌가 / 보관하기 때문에 / 이것을 / 모든 다른 점심들과 함께 / 당신이 / 먹었던 / 또 다른 점심으로.

의역 해석

당신의 점심에 대한 기억이 사라진 것 까지는 아니다. 만약 어디서 먹었는지, 누구와 먹었는지 같은 적절한 단서가 주어지면 당신은 먹었던 것을 기억할 것이다. 그렇다기 보다는, 지난주 점심에 먹은 것을 기억하는 것이 어려운 것이다. 왜냐하면 당신의 뇌는 이것을 다른 모든 당신이 먹었던 점심들과 함께 그냥 또 하나의 점심이라고 보관하기 때문이다.

Unit 4 4형식 P.44

53. In an open discussion / designed / to solve / problems, the discussion group leader / should give / group members / a chance / to make suggestions / before making / his own.

직독직해 해석

열린 토론에서 / 설계된 / 해결하기 위해 / 문제들을, / 토론 그룹 리더는 / 주어야만 한다 / 그룹 멤버들에게 / 기회를 / 제안할 / 하기 전에 / 그 자신의

의역 해석

문제를 해결하기 위해 설계된 열린 토론에서, 토론 그룹 리더는 자신의 제안을 하게 전에 맴버들에게 제안할 기회를 줘야만 한다.

54. By giving / Apocalypse Now / a setting / that was contemporary / at the time of its release, / audiences / were able to experience / and identify / with its themes / more easily / than they / would have / if the film / had been a literal adaptation / of the novel.

직독직해 해석

줌으로써 / Apocalypse Now에게 / 환경을 / 동시대의 / 출판의 시기와, / 관중들은 / 경험할 수 있었고 / 동일시할 수 있었습니다 / 이것의 주제와 / 더 쉽게 / 그것이 / 그랬을 것 보다 / 영화가 / 글자 그대로의 각색이었을 때 / 소설의

의역 해석

Apocalypse Now에게 출판하는 시기와 동시대의 환경을 줌으로써, 관중들은 이 영화가 소설의 글자그대로의 각색이었을 때 그랬을 것 보다 더 쉽게 이것의 주제를 경험하고 주제와 동일시할 수 있었습니다.

55. However, / we / can anticipate / that personal growth and performance / will progress / faster / in young, developing athletes / who are given / mental skills training / than in athletes / not exposed to MST.

직독직해 해석

그러나, / 우리는 / 예상할 수 있습니다 / 개인적인 성장과 수행능력이 / 발전할 것이라고 / 더 빠르게 / 어리고, 발전하는 운동선수에게서 / 받은 / 정신 기술 훈련을 / 운동선수에게서보다 / MST에 노출되지 않은.

의역 해석

그러나 우리는 MST에 노출되지 않은 운동선수에게서 보다 MST를 받은 어리고 발전하는 운동선수가 더 빠르게 발전할 것이라고 예상할 수 있습니다.

56. Psychologists / who study / giving behavior / have noticed / that some people / give / substantial amounts / to one or two charities, / while others / give / small amounts / to many charities.

직독직해 해석

심리학자들은 / 연구하는 / 기부하는 행동을 / 알아차렸다 / 몇몇 사람들이 / 준다는 것을 / 상당한(많은) 양을 / 하나 혹은 두 자선단체에, / 반면에 다른 사람들은 / 준다 / 작은 양을 / 많은 자선단체들에.

의역 해석

기부하는 행동을 연구하는 심리학자들은 몇몇 사람들은 많은 양을 한 두 단체에 주고 다른 사람들은 작은 양을 많은 자선단체들에 준다는 것을 알았다.

57. I / asked / my friends / what they / would do / to change / the world / if they / could.

직독직해 해석

저는 / 물었습니다 / 제 친구들에게 / 그들이 / 무엇을 할 것인지 / 바꾸기 위해 / 세상을 / 만약 그들이 / 할 수 있다면.

의역 해석

저는 제 친구들에게 만약 그들이 바꿀 수 있다면 세상을 바꾸기 위해 무엇을 할 것인지를 물었습니다.

58. Think / about the pressure / associated / with having to convince / the other party / we / are right / when we / thinks / we / are wrong.

직독직해 해석

생각해봐라 / 압박에 대해 / 관련된 / 확신시켜야만 하는 것과 / 다른 상대방에게 / 우리가 옳다는 것을 / 우리가 / 생각할 때 / 우리가 / 잘못되었다고.

의역 해석

우리도 우리가 틀렸다고 생각을 할 때 상대방에게 우리가 옳다는 것을 확신시켜야만 하는 것에 관련된 압박에 대해서 생각해봐라.

59. By giving / yourself / freedom / to follow / your intuition, / you / develop / your sensitivity / to your inner voice.

직독직해 해석

줌으로써 / 스스로에게 / 자유를 / 따를 / 당신의 직관을, / 당신은 / 개발한다 / 당신의 민감성을 / 당신의 내면의 목소리에 대한.

의역 해석

스스로에게 당신의 직관을 따를 자유를 줌으로써 당신은 내부 목소리에 대한 민감성을 개발한다.

60. In 1513, / Machiavelli / had acknowledged / in Il principe / that citizens / might have / a right / to 'think / all things, speak / all things, write / all things,; / but insisted / that the prince / was always equally entitled / to deny / them / this privilege.

직독직해 해석

1513년에 / 마키아벨리는 / 인정했다 / 군주론2에서 / 시민들이 / 가지고 있을지도 모른다는 것을 / 권리를 / 생각할 / 모든 것을, / 말할 / 모든 것을 / 쓸 / 모든 것을, / 그러나 주장했다 / 왕은 / 항상 동등하게 권한을 부여받는다고 / 주지 않을 수 있는 / 그들에게 / 이러한 특권을.

의역 해석

1513년도에 마키아벨리는 군주론2에서 시민들이 모든 것을 생각하고 말하고 쓸 권리를 가지고 있을지도 모른다고 주장은 했지만, 동시에 왕은 시민들에게 이러한 특권을 주지 않을 수 있는 권한을 부여받았다고 주장했다.

61. Experiment and observation / provide / us / with clues, / but the clues / are cryptic, / and require / some considerable ingenuity / to solve.

직독직해 해석

실험과 관찰은 / 제공한다 / 우리에게 / 단서들을, / 그러나 단서들은 / 애매하다, / 그리고 요구한다 / 몇몇 상당한 독창성을 / 해결하기 위한.

의역 해석

실험과 관찰은 우리에게 단서를 제공하지만 단서들은 애매하고 해결하기 위해선 상당한 독창성을 필요로 한다.

62. Human intelligence / makes use of / very effective pruning techniques / that prevent / the brain / from running / in overdrive, / attempting / to process / billions of potential situations / of which only one or two / might be useful. / The expense / of this brute computational approach / is simply not suited / to biological beings. / However, / what is clear / is that the availability / of practically infinite mathematical ability, / and abundant calculating speed, / do result in / discoveries / that our biological brains / have not yet made.

직독직해 해석

인간의 지능은 / 사용한다 / 매우 효과적인 가지치기 기술들을 / 막아주는 / 뇌가 / 작동하는 것을 / 과하게, / 시도하면서 / 처리하는 것을 / 수십억의 잠재적 상황을 / 겨우 하나 두 개만이 / 유용할지도 모르는. / 비용은 / 이러한 잔혹한 계산적 접근법의 / 단순히 맞지 않는다 / 생물학적 존재들에게. / 그런데, / 분명한 것은 / 이용가능성이 / 실용적으로 무한한 수학적 능력의, / 그리고 풍부한 계산 속도의 / 야기시킨다 / 발견을 / 우리의 생물학적 뇌가 / 아직 하지 못한.

의역 해석

인간의 지능은 뇌가 과하게 작동하는 것을 막아주는 매우 효과적인 가지치기 기술들을 사용한다. 그러면서 그들은 한 두 개만이 유용할 지도 모르는 잠재적 상황을 처리하는 것을 시도한다. 이러한 잔혹한 계산적 접근법의 단순히 생물학적 존재들에겐 맞지 않는다. 그러나 분명한 것은 실용적으로 무한한 수학적 능력의 이용가능성과 풍부한 계산 속도는 우리의 뇌가 하지 하지 못했단 발견을 야기시킨다.

Unit 5 5형식 P.52

63. Because of his injury, / Jim / wasn't able to play / on the basketball team / during the rest of that year, / but the coach / did make / him / equipment manager / so that he / could come and practice.

직독직해 해석

그의 부상 때문에, / 짐은 / 플레이할 수 없었습니다 / 농구팀에서 / 그 해의 나머지 기간 동안 / 그러나 코치는 / 만들었다 / 그를 / 장비 관리인으로 / 그가 / 와서 연습할 수 있도록.

의역 해석

그의 부상 때문에 짐은 농구팀에서 그 해 나머지 기간 동안 플레이할 수 없었습니다, 하지만 코치는 그가 와서 연습할 수 있도록 그를 장비 매니저로 임명했습니다.

64. Composers / describe / their private world / through the use of sound. / Making / such a description / concrete and detailed / requires / not just inspiration / but certain practical tools and skills.

직독직해 해석

작곡가들은 / 묘사한다 / 그들의 사적인 세계를 / 소리의 사용을 통해. / 만드는 것은 / 그러한 묘사를 / 구체적이고 상세하게 / 필요로 한다 / 영감 뿐만 아니라 / 특정한 실용적인 도구와 기술들을.

의역 해석

작곡가들은 소리의 사용을 통해 자신들의 사적인 세상을 묘사한다. 그러한 묘사를 구체적이고 상세하게 만들어주는 것은 영감 뿐만 아니라 특정한 실용적인 도구와 기술들이 필요하다.

65. Medicine / comes / in lots of different packages. / Painkillers / in tablet / can make / your headache / go away. / Antibiotic cream / from a tube / can prevent / your cuts / from becoming infected.

직독직해 해석

약은 / 나온다 / 다양한 패키지로. / 진통제는 / 알약에 있는 / 할 수 있다 / 당신의 두통이 / 사라지게. / 항생제 크림은 / 튜브로부터의 / 막을 수 있다 / 당신의 상처가 / 감염되는 것을.

의역 해석

약은 다양한 패키지로 나온다. 알약에 있는 진통제는 당신의 두통이 사라지게 할 수 있다. 튜브로부터의 항생제 크림은 당신의 상처가 감염되는 것을 막을 수 있다.

66. Empower / people / by letting / them / know / that you / believe in / them / and allowing / them / to take action.

직독직해 해석

권한을 부여해라 / 사람들에게 / 그들이 / 알게함으로써 / 당신이 / 믿는다는 것을 / 그들을 / 그리고 가능하게 함으로써 / 그들이 / 조치를 취하는 것을.

의역 해석

사람들에게 당신이 믿는다는 것을 알게 하고 그들이 조치를 취하는 것을 허락하는 것과 같은 방식으로 사람들에게 권한을 부여해라.

67. For books, / there are various filters / that help / readers / distinguish / between reliable and unreliable information.

직독직해 해석

책들에 대해서, / 다양한 필터들이 있다 / 돕는 / 독자들이 / 구별하는 것을 / 믿을 수 있는 정보와 믿을 수 없는 정보를

의역 해석

책들에 대해서, 독자들이 믿을 수 있는 정보와 믿을 수 없는 정보를 구별하는 것을 돕는 다양한 필터들이 있다.

68. As Tom / was waiting for / a bus, / he / noticed / a blind man / trying / to cross / the street. / The traffic / was heavy, / and it was likely the blind man / would get hit, / as he / was not crossing / at a crosswalk.

직독직해 해석

톰이 / 기다리고 있을 때 / 버스를, / 그는 / 보았다 / 한 눈이 안 보이시는 분이 / 노력하는걸 / 건너기 위해서 / 길을. / 교통은 / 혼잡했다, / 그리고 그 눈이 안 보이시는 분은 / 차에 치일 가능성이 있었다 / 그가 / 건너고 있지 않았기 때문에 / 횡단보도에서.

의역 해석

톰이 버스를 기다리고 있을 때, 그는 어떤 눈이 안 보이시는 분이 길을 건너기 위해 노력하는걸 보았다. 교통은 혼잡했고 그가 횡단보도에서 건너고 있는 것이 아니었기 때문에 그 눈이 안 보이시는 분은 차에 치일 가능성이 있었다.

69. As anyone / who has ever watched / a parent, a sibling, a spouse / succumb / to the spreading darkness / knows, / there is no way / to stop / the lights / from turning off, / no way / to switch / them / back on / once they've / grown dim.

직독직해 해석

어느 누구라도 / 본 적이 있는 / 부모, 형제, 배우자가 / 굴복하는 것을 / 퍼지는 어둠에 / 알 듯이, / 방법이 없다 / 막을 수 있는 / 불빛이 / 꺼지는 것을, / 방법이 없다 / 켤 수 있는 / 그것들을 / 일단 그것들이 / 희미해지게 되면.

의역 해석

부모, 형제, 배우자가 퍼지는 어둠에 굴복하는 것을 본 적이 있는 어느 누구라도 알 듯이, 그 불빛이 꺼지는 것을 막을 수 있는 방법은 없고, 일단 희미해지면 그것들을 다시 켤 수 있는 방법도 없다.

70. The combustion / of oxygen / that keeps / us / alive and active / sends out / by-products / called oxygen free radicals.

직독직해 해석

연소는 / 산소의 / 유지해주는 / 우리를 / 살아있고 활동적인 채로 / 방출한다 / 부산물을 / 활성산소라고 불리는.

의역 해석

우리를 살아있고 활동적인 채로 두는 산소의 연소는 활성산소라고 불리는 부산물을 방출한다.

71. A proportion of agricultural land / is left completely uncultivated / so that species/ can gradually colonize / it.

직독직해 해석

농업용 땅의 일부는 / 완전히 경작되지 않은 채로 남겨져 있다 / 종들이 / 점차적으로 대량 서식할 수 있도록 / 여기에.

의역 해석

농업용 땅의 일부는 종들이 여기에 점차적으로 대량서식할 수 있도록 완전히 경작되지 않은 채로 남겨져 있다.

72. As we / invent / more species / of AI, / we / will be forced / to surrender / more / of what is supposedly unique / about humans. / Each step of surrender / — we / are not the only mind / that can play / chess, / fly / a plane, make / music, / or invent / a mathematical law / — will be painful and sad.

직독직해 해석

우리가 / 발명하면서 / 더 많은 종들을 / AI의, / 우리는 / 강요받을 것이다 / 포기하도록 / 더 많은 것을 / 아마 특별했던 것의 / 인간에 대한. / 포기의 각 단계는 / 즉 우리가 / 유일한 정신이 아니라는 / 플레이할 수 있는 / 체스를, / 날릴 수 있는 / 비행기를 / 만들 수 있는 / 음악을, / 혹은 발명할 수 있는 / 수학적 법칙을 / 고통스럽고 슬플 것이다.

의역 해석

우리가 더 많은 AI 종들을 발명하면서 우리는 인간에게만 특별했던 더 많은 것들을 포기하도록 강요받을 것이다. 우리가 수학적 법칙을 만들고, 음악을 만들고, 비행기를 날리고, 체스를 플레이 할 수 있는 유일한 정신이 아니라는 포기의 각 단계는 고통스럽고 슬플 것이다.

73. Because the glow of meteors' burning / makes / them / visible, / people / often call / them / shooting stars.

직독직해 해석

유성의 타는 불빛이 / 만들기 때문에 / 그것을 / 눈에 보이게. / 사람들은 / 종종 부른다 / 그것들을 / 슈팅스타라고.

의역 해석

유성의 타는 불빛이 그것을 눈에 보이게 만들기 때문에, 사람들은 그것들을 슈팅 스타라고 부른다.

74. We / regard / butterfly wings / as being colorful / which are so pretty / that many designers / always want / to use / them / as their sources.

직독직해 해석

우리는 / 여긴다 / 나비의 날개를 / 다채롭다고 / 너무나도 예뻐서 / 많은 디자이너들이 / 항상 원하는 / 사용하기를 / 그것들을 / 그들의 원천으로.

의역 해석

우리는 너무 예뻐서 많은 디자이너들이 항상 자신들의 원천으로 사용하기를 원하는 나비의 날개를 다채롭다고 여긴다.

75. Forcing / your children / to eat, / especially if they / don't like / what is on the plate, / is completely counterproductive.

직독직해 해석

강요하는 것은 / 당신의 아이들이 / 먹도록, / 특히 그들이 / 좋아하지 않을 때 / 쟁반 위에 있는 것을, / 완전히 비생산적이다.

의역 해석

당신의 아이들이 먹도록 강요하는 것은, 특히 쟁반 위에 있는 것을 좋아하지 않을 때, 완전히 비생산적이다.

76. The new bill / obliges / the public sector / to reserve / more than a 3-percent share / for job applicants / aged between 15 and 29 / from next year.

직독직해 해석

새로운 법안은 / 의무로 한다 / 공공 영역이 / 비축하도록 / 3퍼센트 이상의 자리를 / 구직자들을 위해 / 15세에서 29세 사이 나이대의 / 내년부터.

의역 해석

새로운 법안은 공공 부분이 내년부터 15세에서 29세 사이의 구직자들을 위해 3퍼센트 이상의 자리를 마련해두는 것을 의무로 한다.

77. Knowing / the value / of your time / enables / you / to make / wise decision / about where and how you / spend / it / so you / can make the most of / this limited resource / according to your circumstances, goals, and interests.

직독직해 해석

아는 것은 / 가치를 / 당신의 시간의 / 가능하게 한다 / 당신이 / 하는 것을 / 현명한 결정을 / 어디에서 그리고 어떻게 당신이 / 소비할지에 대한 / 그것을 / 당신이 / 가장 잘 이용할 수 있도록 / 이 제한된 자원을 / 당신의 상황, 목표, 그리고 흥미에 따라.

의역 해석

당신의 시간의 가치를 아는 것은 당신이 당신의 상황, 목표, 그리고 흥미에 따라 이 제한된 자원을 가장 잘 이용할 수 있도록 어디에서 그리고 어떻게 당신이 이것을 소비할 지에 대한 현명한 결정을 하는 것을 가능하게 한다.

78. It's utterly possible / that new technological breakthroughs / will make it possible / to find / new oil fields / faster / than we do today, / or to pump / oil / from places / that we can't today.

직독직해 해석

완전히 가능하다 / 새로운 기술적 발전들이 / 가능하게 만들 것이라는 것은 / 발견하는 것을 / 새로운 유전을 / 더 빠른 / 우리가 오늘날 하는 것 보다 / 또는 끌어올리는 것을 / 기름을 / 장소로부터 / 우리가 지금은 할 수 없는.

의역 해석

새로운 기술적 발전들이 오늘날 보다 더 빠른 유전 장소를 찾는 것을 가능하게 만들고 우리가 지금은 할 수 없는 장소에서 기름을 끌어올리는 것을 가능하게 만들 것이라는 것은 완전히 가능한 이야기이다.

79. There are / some people / who believe / that no one / should be trusted. / They / usually feel / this way / because their behavior / compels / others / to lie / to them. / In other words, / they / make it difficult / for others / to tell / them / the truth / because they / respond / rudely or emotionally / to people / who tell / the truth.

직독직해 해석

있다 / 몇몇 사람들이 / 믿는 / 어느 누구도 / 믿어져서는 안된다고. / 그들은 / 보통 느낀다 / 이러한 방식으로 / 왜냐하면 그들의 행동이 / 강요하기 때문에 / 다른 사람들이 / 거짓말하도록 / 그들에게. / 다시 말해서, / 그들은 / 어렵게 만든다 / 다른 사람들이 / 말하는 것을 / 그들에게 / 진실을 / 왜냐하면 그들은 / 반응하기 때문에 / 무례하거나 감정적으로 / 사람들에게 / 말하는 / 진실을.

의역 해석

아무도 믿어선 안된다고 믿는 몇몇 사람들이 있다. 그들이 보통 이런 식으로 느끼는 이유는 그들의 행동이 다른사람들로 하여금 그들에게 거짓말하도록 강요하기 때문이다. 다시 말해서, 그들은 진실을 말해주는 사람들에게 감정적이고 무례하게 반응하기 때문에 다른 사람들이 그들에게 진실을 말해주는 것을 어렵게 만든다.

80. With the coming / of the Industrial Revolution, / the social concentration / of activities / of the public square and indeed the entire public realm / has diminished. Technological innovations / including the telephone and the Internet combined in the latest cell phone innovations / are partly responsible. / The automobile / has made it possible / to travel / in virtual privacy / and thus withdraw / from contact / with others / in trains, buses, and other forms of public transportation.

직독직해 해석

도래로 인해 / 산업 혁명의, / 사회적 집중도는 / 활동의 / 공공 장소와 전체적인 공공 영역의 / 줄어들었다. / 기술 혁신들은 / 최근 핸드폰 혁신에서 합쳐진 인터넷과 전화를 포함하는 / 부분적으로 책임이 있다. / 자동차는 / 가능하게 만들었다 / 이동하는 것을 / 가상 사생활에서 / 따라서 물러나는 것을 / 접촉으로부터 / 다른 사람들과의 / 기차, 버스 그리고 다른 형태의 대중교통에서.

의역 해석

산업 혁명이 도래함으로 인해, 대중들의 광장과 공공 영역의 활동 집중도가 줄어들었다. 최근 핸드폰 혁명에서 합쳐진 인터넷과 전화를 포함한 기술 혁신들은 부분적으로 책임이 있다. 자동차는 가상의 사생활 영역에서 이동하는 것을 가능하게 만들었고 그에 따라 기차, 버스, 그리고 기타 다른 대중교통에서 사람들과의 접촉을 막아주는 것을 가능하게 만들었다.

81. A round coin / is seen / as round / even when viewed / from an angle / at which, objectively, / it / should appear elliptical. / In the same way, / we / see / car wheels / as round, / even though the retinal image / is oval / when viewed / from an angle / other than directly from the front.

직독직해 해석

둥근 동전은 / 여겨진다 / 둥글다고 / 심지어 보여질 때에도 / 각도로부터 / 객관적으로 / 이것이 / 타원형인 것처럼 보여야 하는. / 마찬가지로, / 우리는 / 여긴다 / 자동차의 바퀴들을 / 둥글다고, / 비록 망막의 이미지가 / 타원형일지라도 / 보여질 때 / 각도로부터 / 직접적으로 정면으로부터와는 다른.

의역 해석

둥근 동전은 심지어 객관적으로 타원형인 것처럼 보이는 각도로부터 보여질 때도 둥글다고 여겨진다. 마찬가지로, 우리는 정면으로부터 볼때와는 다른 각도로부터 보여질 때 망막에 맺히는 이미지가 타원형일지라도 자동차 바퀴를 둥글다고 여긴다.

82. For example, / an infant / may point to / Daddy's chair / as a reference / to the absent daddy. / This type of pointing / can be seen / as a transition / from using / pointing / as a proto-demonstrative / with a temporary meaning / to using / pointing / symbolically / with a more permanent meaning.

직독직해 해석

예를 들어, / 아기는 / 가리킬 수 있다 / 아빠의 의자를 / 언급으로 / 아빠가 없는 것에 대한. / 이러한 종류의 지적은 / 여겨질 수 있다 / 전환으로 / 사용하는 것으로부터 / 지적을 / 초기의 지시사로 / 일시적 의미를 가진 / 사용하는 것으로의 / 지적을 / 상징적으로 / 더 영구적인 의미를 가진.

의역 해석

예를 들어, 아기는 아빠가 없다는 것을 나타내주려고 아빠의 의자를 가리킬 수 있다. 이런 종류의 가리킴은 가리키는 것을 일시적 의미를 가진 초기의 지시사로 사용하는 것으로부터 더 영구적인 의미를 가진 상징적인 포인팅으로 사용하는 쪽으로의 변화로 여겨실 수 있다.

83. It is helpful / to think of / sports / as an art form /—as a performing art. / Sports / share / with other cultural expressions / an appeal / to the emotions, aesthetics, drama, entertainment, and inspiration. / The athlete / can be considered / an artist / with a certain amount of self-expression and spontaneity.

직독직해 해석

도움이 된다 / 여기는 것은 / 스포츠를/ 예술의 형태로 / 즉 수행하는 예술로. / 스포츠는 / 공유한다 / 다른 문화적 표현들과 / 호소력을 / 감정, 미학, 드라마, 엔터네이먼트, 그리고 영감에 / 운동선수는 / 여겨질 수 있다 / 예술가로 / 특정한 양의 자기 표현과 즉흥성을 지닌.

의역 해석

스포츠를 예술의 형태로, 즉 수행하는 예술로 여기는 것은 도움이 된다. 스포추는 감정, 미학, 드라마, 엔터테이먼트, 그리고 영감에 대한 호소력을 다른 문화적 표현들과 공유한다. 운동선수는 어느 정도 자기 표현과 즉흥성을 지닌 예술가로 여겨질 수 있다.

84. Within the philosophical disciplines, / logic / must be learned / through the use of examples and actual problem solving. / Only after some time and struggle / does the student / begin / to develop / the insights and intuitions / that enable / him / to see / the centrality and relevance / of this mode of thinking.

직독직해 해석

철학적인 규율들 내에서, / 논리는 / 배워져야만 한다 / 예시의 사용과 실제 문제 해결을 통해서. / 몇몇 시간과 노력이 지나고 나서야 / 비로소 학생은 / 시작할 수 있다 / 개발하는 것을 / 통찰력과 직관을 / 가능하게 해주는 / 그가 / 보는 것을 / 확실성과 적절성을 / 이러한 생각 방식의

의역 해석

철학적인 규율들 내에서, 논리는 예시의 사용과 실제 문제 해결을 통해서 배워져야 한다. 약간의 시간과 노력이 지나고 나서야 비로소 그 학생은 그가 이러한 생각 방식의 중심성과 적절성을 보는 것을 가능하게 해주는 통찰력과 직관을 개발하는 것을 시작할 수 있다.

85. When I / asked / a sales person / to map / his sales performance, / he / was amazed / to see / that he / had achieved / a 5% to 10% annual increase / in sales / while at his firm.

직독직해 해석

내가 / 요청했을 때 / 영업 사원이 / 조사하도록 / 그의 판매 실적을, / 그는 / 놀랐습니다 / 알아서 / 그가 / 성취했다는 것을 / 5~10% 매년 성장을 / 판매에서 / 회사에 있는 동안.

의역 해석

내가 영업사원으로 하여금 자신의 판매 실적을 조사하도록 요청했을 때, 그는 그가 회사에 있는 동안 판매 실적이 매년 5~10% 상승했다는 것을 알아서 놀랐습니다.

Part 2 문제 해설

Unit 1 도치 구문

P.70

1. More important / than success, / which generally means / promotion or / an increase in salary, / is the happiness / which can only be found / in doing work / that one enjoys / for its own sake / and not merely for the rewards / it brings.

직독직해 해석

더 중요한 것은 / 성공보다 / 일반적으로 의미하는 / 승진 또는 / 월급의 증가를 / 행복이다 / 단지 발견될 수 있는 / 일을 할 때 / 한 사람이 즐기는 / 그 자체로 / 보상을 위해서 뿐만 아니라 / 이것이 가져오는

의역 해석

일반적으로 승진 또는 월급의 증가를 의미하는 성공보다 더 중요한 것은 그것이 주는 보상을 위해서 뿐만 아니라 그자체로 즐기는 일을 할 때에만 발견될 수 있는 행복이다.

2. In the center of the room / was the strangest lady / I had ever seen, / sitting at a table.

직독직해 해석

방 가운데에서 / 이상한 여인이 있었다 / 내가 이제껏 본 사람들 중에 / 식탁에 앉은채로

의역 해석

방 가운데에 내가 이제껏 본 사람 중에 가장 이상한 여인이 식탁에 앉아 있었다.

3. So strong / was the emotion / that the brain / rejected / evidence / of the continued existence of / normal, / everyday life / that might have eased it.

직독직해 해석

너무도 강력한 것은 / 감정이다 / 그래서 뇌는 / 거부했다 / 증거를 / 지속적인 존재에 대한 / 정상적이고 / 매일의 삶의 / 이것을 완화 시켰을지도 모르는

의역 해석

너무나도 강력한 것은 감정이어서 뇌는 이러한 감정을 완화 시켰을지도 모르는 매일의 정상적인 존재에 대한 지속적인 증거를 거부했다.

4. Most helpful / to the calm and peaceful atmosphere / that the two-year-old child needs / but cannot produce / for himself/herself / is the presence of comforting music,/ in almost any form.

직독직해 해석

성장은 / 항상 가장자리에 있다 / 딱 경계선 밖에 / 너가 있는 장소의 / 현재.

의역 해석

성장은 항상 가장자리에, 즉 너가 현재 있는 장소의 딱 경계선 밖에 있다.

5. Things / we thought / we wanted most intensely, / we realize, / we don't care about.

직독직해 해석

것들은 / 우리가 생각하기에 / 우리가 가장 강력하게 원했던 / 우리는 깨달았다 / 우리는 신경 쓰지 않는다.

의역 해석

우리는 우리가 생각하기에 가장 강력하게 원했던 것들을 우리가 신경쓰지 않는 다는 것을 깨달았다.

6. Competition / has made possible / the enormous material progress / of the past 200 years / by unlocking the energies of society.

직독직해 해석

경쟁은 / 가능하게 해왔다 / 거대한 중요한 진보를 / 지난 200년 동안의 / 사회의 에너지들을 열면서

의역 해석

경쟁은 사회의 에너지들을 열면서 지난 200년 동안의 거대하고 중요한 진보를 가능하게 해왔다.

7. The federal government, private research groups, and others / collect and provide / valuable information / and extensive data / on many facets / of economic life, / and the computer / has made possible / speedier and more sophisticated testing of ideas.

직독직해 해석

연방 정부, 개인 연구 그룹들, 그리고 다른 그룹들은 / 모으고 제공한다 / 가치있는 정보를 / 그리고 광범위한 데이터를 / 많은 면에 대한 / 경제적 삶의 / 그리고 컴퓨터는 / 가능하게 만들어왔다 / 더 빠르고 정교한 아이디어들의 테스트를.

의역 해석

연방 정부, 개인 연구 그룹들, 드리고 다른 그룹들은 경제적 삶의 많은 면데 대한 가치있는 정보와 광범위한 데이트를 모으고 제공한다. 그리고 컴퓨터는 아이디어의 더 빠르고 세련된 테스트를 가능하게 만들어왔다.

8. We / have regarded as natural / the body / that our parents gave us — / a fixed, unchanging fact of nature

직독직해 해석

우리는 / 당연하게 여겨왔다 / 몸을 / 우리의 부모님이 우리에게 준 / 고정된, 자연의 변하지 않는 사실로

의역 해석

우리는 우리의 부모님이 우리에게 준 몸을 고정된, 자연의 변하지 않는 사실로 당연하게 여겨왔다.

9. Not until they began / cultivating tobacco / for sale abroad / could they / finance / their activities / and develop / their country.

직독직해 해석

그들이 시작하고 나서야 / 담배를 재배하는 것을 / 해외에 팔려고 / 비로소 그들은 / 돈을 댈 수 있었다 / 그들의 활동에 / 그리고 발달시키는 데에 / 그들의 나라를

의역 해석

그들은 담배를 해외에 팔려고 재배하고 나서야 비로소 그들의 활동에 돈을 댈 수 있었고 그들의 나라를 발전시킬 수 있었다.

10. Lucky lottery winners / or other recipients / of sudden wealth / buy a large house, / fancy furniture, / a new car, etc. / but rarely does the money appear to open / the way / for a more meaningful, exciting existence.

직독직해 해석

운 좋은 복권 당첨자들은 / 또는 다른 수령자들 / 갑작스러운 부의 / 큰 집을 사고, / 화려한 가구를 사고 / 새 차 등등을 산다. / 그러나 거의 돈이 열어주는 것 같지 않다 / 길을 / 더 의미 있고 흥미로운 존재를 위한

의역 해석

운 좋은 복권 당첨자들 또는 갑작스러운 부의 다른 수령자들은 큰 집, 화려한 가구, 새 차 등을 산다. 그러나 돈은 더 의미 있고 흥미로운 존재를 위한 길을 열어주는 것 같지는 않다.

11. Not only does the 'leaf fish' / look like a leaf, / but it also imitates / the movement / of a drifting a leaf underwater.

직독직해 해석

leaf fish 는 / 나뭇잎처럼 보일 뿐만 아니라 / 모방한다 / 움직임을 / 수중에서 흘러가는 잎의

의역 해석

leaf fish는 나뭇잎처럼 생겼을 뿐만 아니라 수중에서 흘러간 는 잎의 움직임을 모방한다.

12. Only then can social policies / be considered / key factors of production, / beyond their role / as instruments of social protection.

직독직해 해석

그때가 되어서야 비로소 사회 정책들은 / 여겨질 수 있다 / 생산의 핵심 요소라고 / 그들의 역할을 넘어서 / 사회적 보호의 수단으로서의

의역 해석

그때가 되어서야 비로소 사회 정책들은 사회적 보호 수단으로서의 역할을 넘어서 생산의 핵심 요소가 여겨질 수 있다.

13. As our incomes and material standards rise, / so do our expected achievements.

직독직해 해석

마치 우리의 소득과 물질 기준이 오르는 것처럼 / 우리의 기대하는 성취도 또한 오른다.

의역 해석

마치 우리의 소득과 물질 기준이 오르는 것처럼 우리의 기대하는 성취도 또한 오른다.

14. The green movement / is sometimes criticized / for downplaying / the cost of going green. / Just as food movements / have sometimes acted / unaware of / the difficulty / of a working-class family / negotiating / not only its food budget but also the effect / on that budget / of the time constraints / of working parents, / so too did the early environmentalism movement / sometimes pay too little attention / to the financial effect / of environmentally responsible behavior.

직독직해 해석

환경친화적인 운동은 / 때때로 비판받는다 / 경시하기 때문에 / 환경친화적이 되는 것의 비용을. / 마치 음식을 위한 운동이 / 때때로 작용하는 것처럼 / 알지 못한채로 / 어려움을 / 서민 계층 가족이 / 타협하는 / 음식 예산 뿐만 아니라 / 영향을 / 예산에 미치는 / 시간 제약의 / 서민 부모들의, / 초기 환경주의 운동 또한 / 때때로 거의 주의를 기울이지 않았다 / 재정적인 영향에 / 환경적으로 책임있는 행동의.

의역 해석

환경 친화적인 운동은 때때로 환경 친화적이 되는 것의 비용을 경시하기 때문에 비판을 받기도 한다. 마치 음식 운동이 서민 부모들이 음식 예산 뿐만 아니라, 시간 제약의 예산에 미치는 영향까지도 타협해야하는 어려움을 알지 못한채로 행해지는 것처럼 환경 친화 운동 또한 때때로 환경적으로 책임있는 행동의 금전적 영향에 대해선 거의 관심을 기울이지 않았다.

15. Truly as the Internet / seems global / these days, / less than half of the world's / has access / to it.

직독직해 해석

비록 진정으로 인터넷은 / 글로벌 한 것 같을지라도 / 오늘날에 / 절반 이하의 세계 나라들은 / 접근할 수 있다 / 그것에

의역 해석

오늘날 비록 인터넷이 글로벌 한 것 같을지라도 오직 절반 이하의 나라들만 인터넷에 접근할 수 있다.

16. No longer were the shores / densely wooded, / nor could I see / any wildlife anywhere

직독직해 해석

더 이상 해변가가 / 빽빽하게 우거지지 않았다 / 나는 볼 수 없었다 / 어떠한 야생동물도

의역 해석

더 이상 해변가가 빽빽하게 우거지지 않았고, 나는 어디서도 야생동물을 볼 수 없었다.

17. So popular / did they / become / that the amount of small change / minted / was inadequate / for the demand / and the coffeehouses and the houses / had to issue / tokens / that were generally acceptable / within the immediate area.

직독직해 해석

너무나도 인기가 있게 / 그것들이 / 되어서 / 작은 잔돈의 양은 / 발생된 / 부적절했다 / 수요에 / 그리고 커피 하우스와 집들은 / 발행해야만 했다 / 토큰들을 / 일반적으로 받아들여질 수 있는 / 이 지역 내에서.

의역 해석

그것들은 너무나도 인기가 있게 되어서 발생되는 작은 잔돈의 양은 수요에 부적합했고, 커피가게들과 집들은 이 지역 내에서 일반적으로 받아들여질 수 있는 토큰(동전대신쓰는 대용물)을 발행해야만 했다.

Unit 2 비교 구문

P.77

18. Scientists / can lessen / bias / by running / as many trials / as possible / and by keeping / accurate notes / of each observation / made.

직독직해 해석

과학자들은 / 줄일 수 있습니다 / 편견을 / 함으로써 / 많은 시도를 / 가능한만큼 많이 / 그리고 / 씀으로써 / 정확한 결과를 / 각 실험의 / 되어진

의역 해석

과학자들은 많은 시도를 가능한 많이 함으로써, 실행된 각 실험의 정확한 결과를 적음으로써 편견을 줄일 수 있습니다.

19. At the end of the round of introductions, / the students / were asked / to write down / the names / of as many other students / as they could remember.

직독직해 해석

소개 단계의 끝에서 / 학생들은 / 요청받았다 / 적도록 / 이름을 / 많은 다른 학생들의 / 그들이 기억할 수 있는만큼

의역 해석

소개 단계의 끝에서 학생들은 최대한 기억할 수 있을 만큼 많이 다른 학생들의 이름을 적도록 요청받았다.

20. You / are under the false impression / that you / do not have / as many items / to pack / as you really do.

직독직해 해석

너는 / 잘못된 인상 하에 있다 / 너가 / 가지고 있지 않다는 / 많은 품목들을 / 쌀만한 / 실제로 너가 그런 것과는 달리

의역 해석

너는 실제와는 달리 너가 짐을 쌀 만한 품목을 가지고 있지 않다는 잘못된 인상 하에 있다.

21. Time itself / remains unchanged / in the sense that it carries on / in the same way / as it has / for millions of years.

직독직해 해석

시간 그 자체는 / 변하지 않는 채로 있다 / 이것이 계속해서 움직인다는 점에 있어서 / 같은 방식으로 / 이것이 움직이는 / 수백만년 동안

의역 해석

수백만년 동안 같은 방식으로 움직여 왔다는 점에 있어서 시간은 변하지 않고 계속 간다.

22. The number of researchers / per 1,000 people / in the EAP / in 2007 / was twice as large as that / in 1999.

직독직해 해석

연구자들의 수는 / 천명당 / EAP에서 / 2007년에 / 두배 더 크다 / 1999년도 보다

의역 해석

EAP에서 2007년의 천명당 연구자들의 수는 1999년보다 두 배 더 많다.

23. The more intelligent you are, / the more you may be inclined to consider rapidly / many factors / before making a decision.

직독직해 해석

너가 더 똑똑할수록, / 너가 더 빠르게 고려하는 경향이 있을지도 모른다. / 많은 요소들을 / 결정을 하기 전에

의역 해석

너가 더 똑똑할수록 결정하기 전에 많은 요소들을 빠르게 고려하는 경향이 있을지도 모른다.

24. When a small butterfly / was caught unmercifully / in a thornbush, / the more the butterfly / struggled to free itself, / the deeper / the thorns / cut into its fragile body.

직독직해 해석

작은 나비가 / 무자비하게 잡혔을 때 / 가시덤불 안에 / 나비가 / 스스로를 자유롭게하려고 더 노력할수록 / 더 깊어진다 / 가시가 / 연약한 몸을 찌르는 것이

의역 해석

작은 나비가 가시덤불 안에 무자비하게 잡혔을 때 스스로를 자유롭게 하려고 더 노력할수록 가시가 연약한 몸을 찌르는 것이 더 깊어진다.

25. The more effectively they communicate / that authority, / the more secure / the child feels, / and the better / able he is to move / away from them / toward a life of his own.

직독직해 해석

그들이 더 효과적으로 전달할수록 / 그 권한을 / 더 안전해진다 / 아이들이 느끼기에 / 그리고 더 좋아진다 / 그는 더 잘 움직일 수 있다 / 그들로부터 멀어져서 / 그들만의 삶을 향해

의역 해석

그들(부모님)이 더 효과적으로 그 권한을 전달할수록 아이들은 더 안전함을 느낀다. 그리고 부모님으로부터 멀어져서 자신만의 삶을 위해 더 잘 움직일 수 있다.

26. One of the little understood paradoxes / in communication / is that the more difficult the word, / the shorter the explanation.

직독직해 해석

거의 이해되지 않는 역설들중에 하나는 / 의사소통에서 / 단어가 더 어려울수록 / 설명은 더 짧아진다는 것이다.

의역 해석

의사소통에서 거의 이해되지 않는 역설들 중에 하나는 단어가 더 어려울수록 설명은 더 짧아진다는 것이다.

27. The higher the economic distance, / the higher the resistance / for that destination / and, consequently, / the lower the demand.

직독직해 해석

경제적인 거리가 멀어질수록 / 저항도가 높아진다 / 그 목적지에 대한 / 그리고 결과적으로 / 수요가 낮아진다.

의역 해석

경제적인 거리가 멀어질수록 그 목적지에대한 저항도가 높아지고 결과적으로 수요는 낮아진다.

28. His morality / was severely bruised / due to the bribery scandal. / And people's anger / became all the more intense / because he / just told lies / about the case / in a desperate bid / to avoid criminal charges.

직독직해 해석

그의 도덕성은 / 심각하게 문제가 생겼다 / 스캔들 때문에 / 그리고 사람들의 화는 / 더 강렬해졌다 / 그가 / 거짓말을 했기 때문에 / 사건에 대해 / 필사적인 노력을 / 범죄의 책임을 피하기 위해

의역 해석

스캔들 때문에 그의 도덕성에는 심각한 문제가 생겼다. 그리고 그가 범죄의 책임을 피하기 위해 필사적인 노력을 하며 사건에 대해 거짓말을 했기 때문에 사람들은 더 분노했다.

29. There is often no more effective way / to help people / understand / the message / than to have it modeled / for them / by the manager.

직독직해 해석

더 이상 효과적인 방법은 없다 / 사람들을 돕는 / 이해하도록 / 메시지를 / 본보기를 보여주는 것 보다 / 그들을 위해 / 매니저에 의해

의역 해석

매니저가 그들을 위해 본보기가 되어주는 것보다 사람들이 메시지를 이해하도록 돕는 효과적인 방법은 없다.

30. There are no qualities / that an officer / must possess / as important as loyalty.

직독직해 해석

어떠한 특징도 없다 / 공직자가 / 소유해야만 하는 / 충성도만큼 중요한

의역 해석

공직자가 가져야하는 가장 중요한 것은 충성도이다.

31. Nothing is as important / as our citizens' safety, / so fixing / this broken traffic lights / should be made a top priority.

직독직해 해석

어떤것도 중요하지 않다 / 우리 시민들의 안전보다 / 그래서 고치는 것은 / 이 고장난 신호등을 / 최고의 우선순위가 되어야만 한다.

의역 해석

우리 시민들의 안전이 가장 중요하기 때문에 이 고장난 신호등을 고치는 것이 최고의 우선순위가 되어야만 한다.

32. The report / about Africa's potential / says / that during the past five years, / Africa / has seen more growth / in mobile service subscriptions / than any other region / in the world.

직독직해 해석

보고서는 / 아프리카 잠재력에 대한 / 말한다 / 지난 오년동안 / 아프리카는 / 성장을 보여왔다 / 모바일 서비스 이용에 있어서 / 어느 지역보다 / 세계에 있는

의역 해석

아프리카의 잠재력에 대한 보고서는 지난 오년동안 모바일 서비스 이용에 있어서 세계 어느 지역보다 아프리카가 가장 많은 성장을 했다고 말한다.

33. Journeys / are the midwives of thought. / Few places / are more conducive / to internal conversations / than a moving plane, ship, or train.

직독직해 해석

여행은 / 생각의 산파이다. / 거의 어떠한 장소도 / 내적인 대화에 좋지 않다 / 움직이는 비행기, 배, 기차보다

의역 해석

여행은 생각에 도움을 준다. 움직이는 비행기, 배, 기차보다 내적인 대화에 좋은 장소는 없다.

34. In this digital age, / images / are essential units of information, / and knowing / how to use / photography effectively / is more important / than ever.

직독직해 해석

이러한 디지털 시대에 / 이미지들은 / 정보의 필수적인 단위이다 / 그리고 아는 것은 / 어떻게 사용하는지 / 사진술을 효과적으로 / 가장 중요하다 / 그 어느 때보다

의역 해석

이러한 디지털 시대에 이미지들은 정보의 필수적인 단위이다. 그리고 사진술을 효과적으로 사용하는 방법을 아는 것은 그 어느 때보다 중요하다.

35. I was a coward; / and the thing / I feared more than anything / in the world / was to break up in the battle / and give way to that cowardice.

직독직해 해석

나는 겁쟁이였다 / 그리고 내가 무서워했던 것은 / 그 어떤 것 보다 / 세상에서 / 전쟁에서 패배하는 것이다 / 그리고 겁에 굴복하는 것이다.

의역 해석

나는 겁쟁이였다. 그리고 내가 세상의 그 어떤 것 보다 무서워했던 것은 전쟁에서 패배하는 것과 겁에 굴복하는 것이었다.

36. Even the most determined of parents / can find / it / a challenge / to encourage their child / not to spend too long sitting / in front of the television or computer.

직독직해 해석

심지어 가장 단호한 부모님들일지라도 / 생각한다 / 그것이 / 어렵다고 / 그들의 아이들을 격려하는 것이 / 너무 오래 앉아 있지 말라고 / TV나 컴퓨터 앞에

의역 해석

심지어 가장 단호한 부모님들 일지라도 아이들에게 TV나 컴퓨터 앞에 너무 오래 앉아있지 말라고 격려하는 것이 어렵다고 생각한다.

37. Architecture / is no more "frozen music" / than music / is "melted architecture."

직독직해 해석

건축은 / 언 음악이 아니다 / 음악이 / 녹은 건축이 아닌 것처럼.

의역 해석

음악이 녹은 건축이 아닌 것처럼 건축은 언 음악이 아니다.

38. Organic farmers / grow crops / that are no less plagued / by pests / than those of conventional farmers.

직독직해 해석

유기농 농부들은 / 작물을 기른다 / 감염된 작물들을 / 해충에 의해 / 전통적인 농부들의 작물들이 그랬던 것처럼

의역 해석

전통적인 농부들이 해충에 감염된 작물들을 기르는 것처럼 유기농 농부들 또한 해충에 감염된 작물들을 기른다.

39. He / is no less diligent / than you, / but he / is not so faithful / to his family / as you.

직독직해 해석

그는 / 부지런하다 / 당신처럼 / 그러나 / 그는 / 충실하진 않다 / 그의 가족에 / 너와는 달리

의역 해석

그는 당신처럼 부지런하지만 당신과는 달리 그의 가족에 충실하지는 않다.

40. It is true / that there are rules / of grammar and syntax / just as in music / there are rules of harmony and counterpoint. / One / can no more write / good English / than one / can compose music, / merely by keeping the rules.

직독직해 해석

당연하다 / 문법과 구문의 규칙이 / 음악에 / 하모니의 규칙이 있는 것처럼. / 한 사람은 / 쓸 수 없다 / 좋은 영어를 / 한 사람이 / 작곡할 수 없는 것처럼 / 단순히 규칙을 지키는 것만으로는

의역 해석

음악에서 화음과 대유법의 규칙이 있는 것처럼 문법과 구문의 규칙이 있는 것은 당연하다. 한 사람이 단순히 규칙을 지킴으로써 좋은 음악을 작곡할 수 없는 것처럼 한 사람은 더 이상 좋은 영어를 쓸 수 없다.

41. Tolstoy / is confident / that the artist / who sincerely expresses / feelings of pride / will pass / those feelings / on to us; / we / can no more escape / than we / could escape / an infectious disease.

직독직해 해석

톨스토이는 / 확신했다 / 예술가가 / 진정으로 표현하는 / 자부심의 감정을 / 넘겨줄 것이라고 / 그러한 감정을 / 우리에게 / 우리는 / 도망칠 수 없다 / 우리가 / 도망칠 수 없는 것처럼 / 감염성의 질병에

의역 해석

톨스토이는 진정으로 자부심을 표현하는 예술가는 우리에게 그러한 감정을 넘겨 줄 것이라고 확신했다. 우리가 감염성의 질병에서 벗어날 수 없는 것처럼 우리는 벗어날 수 없다.

42. A wise person / once told / me / that what's important / is not so much the path / you're on / as the direction / you're headed.

직독직해 해석

명한 사람은 / 한번 말해줬다 / 나에게 / 중요한 것은 / 길이라기 보다는 / 너가 있는 / 방향이다 / 너가 향하는

의역 해석

현명한 사람은 나에게 중요한 것은 내가 있는 길이 아닌 향하는 방향이라고 말해줬다.

43. We / learn / certain things / about the other person / not so much from what he says / as from how he says it, / for whatever we speak / we / cannot avoid / giving our listeners / clues / about our origins / and what sort of person we are.

직독직해 해석

우리는 / 배운다 / 특정한 것들을 / 다른 사람들에 대해 / 그가 말하는 것으로라기보다는 / 그가 말하는 방식으로부터 / 우리가 무엇을 말하던지 간에 / 우리는 / 피할 수 없다 / 우리의 청중에게 주는 것을 / 신호들을 / 우리의 기원에 대해 / 그리고 우리가 어떤 종류의 사람인지에 대해

의역 해석

우리는 다른 사람이 말하는 것으로 라기 보다는 말하는 방식으로부터 그 사람에 대해 특정한 것들을 배운다. 우리가 무엇을 말하던지 간에 우리는 청중들에게 우리의 기원에 대해, 우리가 어떤 사람인지에 대해 신호들을 주는 것을 피할 수 없다.

44. Our nervous system / determines / the complexity of activities / that we / are able to perform. / Animals / with nervous systems / similar to a warm's / cannot play soccer, much less chess.

직독직해 해석

우리의 신경체계는 / 결정해준다 / 활동의 복잡성을 / 우리가 / 수행할 수 있는 / 동물들은 / 신경체계가 있는 / 벌레와 유사한 / 축구를 할 수 없다 / 체스는 말할 것도 없이

의역 해석

우리의 신경체계는 우리가 수행 할 수 있는 활동의 복잡성을 결정해준다. 벌레와 유사한 신경체계를 가지고 있는 동물들은 체스는 말할 것도 없고 축구도 할 수 없다.

Unit 3 분사 구문 P.92

45. Recognizing the healing power of humor, / many hospitals / are starting / to take / laughing matters / seriously.

직독직해 해석

유머의 치유력을 인지한다 / 그러한 많은 병원들은 / 시작하고 있다 / 받아들이기를 / 웃음문제를 / 심각하게

의역 해석

유머의 치유력을 인지한 많은 병원들은 웃음 문제를 심각하게 받아들이기 시작했다.

46. Being careful not to be noticed, / he / let / his eyes / trace / the figure of her face, / Her appearance / was simply enchanting.

직독직해 해석

알아차려지지 않기 위해 조심스럽다 / 그러한 그는 / 하게 했다 / 그의 눈이 / 쫓아가도록 / 그녀의 얼굴을 / 그녀의 외모는 / 단순히 매력적이었다.

의역 해석

알아차려지지 않기 위해 조심한 그는 그의 눈이 그녀의 얼굴을 쫓도록 했다. 그녀의 외모는 단순히 매력적이었다.

47. Asked / about the most and least trustworthy people / in our society, / most of them / answered / professors / are the most trustworthy / and politicians / are the least trustworthy group / in society.

직독직해 해석

질문을 받았다 / 가장 최고로, 가장 적게 믿을만한 사람에 대해 / 우리 사회에서 / 그러한 대부분의 사람들은 / 대답했다 / 교수들이 / 가장 믿을만한 사람이고 / 정치인들이 / 가장 못 믿을만한 사람이라고 / 사회에서

의역 해석

우리 사회에서 가장 믿을만하고 가장 믿지 못할 사람에 대해 질문을 받은 대부분의 사람들은 교수들이 가장 믿을만하고 정치인들이 가장 믿을만하지 않다고 대답했다.

48. Given your experience and expertise, / I / believe / you / would be an ideal person / to speak to them.

직독직해 해석

너의 경험과 전문 지식을 고려해볼 때 / 나는 / 믿는다 / 너가 / 이상적인 사람이 될 것이라고 / 그들에게 말을 할

의역 해석

너의 경험과 전문 지식을 고려해볼 때 나는 너가 그들에게 말을 할 이상적인 사람이 될 것이라고 믿는다.

49. In doing so, / the scientist / reverses / his drive / toward mathematical exactness / in favor of rhetorical vagueness and metaphor, / thus violating / the code of intellectual conduct / that defines him as a scientist.

직독직해 해석

그렇게 함에 있어서 / 과학자들은 / 뒤집어버린다 / 그의 욕구를 / 수학적인 정확성을 추구하는 / 수사학적인 애매함과 은유법을 위해서 / 따라서 위반한다 / 지적인 행동의 코드를 / 그를 과학자로서 정의해주는

의역 해석

수사학적인 애매함과 은유법을 위해서 과학자들은 수학적인 정확설을 추구하는 그들의 욕구를 뒤집어버린다. 따라서 그를 과학자로서 정의해주는 지적인 행동의 코드를 위반한다.

50. These new technologies / have revealed / that many things / can produce / infrasound, / from earthquakes and thunderstorms / to trains / and underground explosions, thus making possible the warning of earthquakes and the monitoring of underground nuclear-explosion tests.

직독직해 해석

이러한 새로운 기술들은 / 밝혀냈다 / 많은 것들이 / 생산할 수 있다는 것을 / 초저주파를 / 지진과 번개로부터 / 기차와 / 지하의 폭발까지 / 따라서 / 가능하게 해준다 / 지진의 경고를 / 그리고 지하 핵폭발 실험의 모니터링을

의역 해석

이러한 새로운 기술들은 지진과 번개로부터 기차와 지하의 폭발까지 많은 것들이 초저주파를 생산할 수 있다는 것을 발견했다. 따라서 지진의 경고와 지하 핵폭발 실험의 모니터링을 가능하게 해줬다.

51. The making of this / requires / the mutual agreement / of two or more persons or parties, / one of them / ordinarily making an offer / and another accepting.

직독직해 해석

이것들을 만드는 것은 / 요구한다 / 상호간 동의를 / 둘이나 그 이상의 사람이나 집단들의 / 그들중 하나는 / 일반적으로 제안하면서 / 그리고 또다른사람이 승낙을 하면서

의역 해석

이것을 만드는 것은 둘 또는 그 이상의 사람이나 집단의 상호 동의를 요구한다. 그들중 하나는 일반적으로 제안하고 또 다른 사람이 승낙을 하면서

52. Suddenly, / the plane / was in the middle of the storm, / jumping and swinging / in the darkness, / the rain / crashing down on the windows / with incredible violence.

직독직해 해석

갑작스럽게 / 비행기는 / 폭풍의 한가운데에 있었다 / 점프하고 흔들리는 / 어둠 속에 / 비는 / 창문에 떨어지는 채로 / 격렬하게

의역 해석

갑작스럽게, 비가 창문에 격렬하게 떨어지는 채로 비행기는 어둠속에서 점프하고 흔들리며 폭풍의 한가운데에 있었다.

53. Jaisalmer / is the only fortress city / in India / still functioning, / with one quarter of its population / living / within the walls.

직독직해 해석

Jaisalmer는 / 유일한 요새 도시이다 / 인도에 / 여전히 작동하는 / 이 인구의 1/4가 / 살고 있는 / 그 벽 안에서

의역 해석

Jaisalmer는 인구의 1/4가 살고 있는 인도에서 여전히 작동하는 유일한 요새 도시이다.

54. With nearly eighty percent of mothers of school-age children / in the work force, / millions of children / are on their own / between 3.p.m and 6 p.m., the hours / when youth are most likely to commit crime / or be victimized by it.

직독직해 해석

거의 학교 갈 나이의 아이를 둔 부모의 80퍼센트가 / 직장에 있는 채로 / 수백만의 아이들은 / 스스로 있는다 / 3시에서 6시에 / 이 시간은 / 어린아이들이 범죄를 저지를 가능성이 큰 / 혹은 그것에 의해 희생될

의역 해석

학교 갈 나이의 아이의 부모의 거의 80퍼센트가 직장에 있고, 아이들은 어린아이들이 가장 범죄를 저지르거나 범죄에 희생될 가능성이 큰 3시에서 6사이에 혼자 있는다.

55. There was no one / in sight / but a girl of about twelve, / with her eyes covered with bandage, / who was being led carefully / between the flower beds / by a little boy. / She stopped, / and evidently asked / who it was that had come in, / and he / seemed to be describing / me / to her.

직독직해 해석

아무도 없었다 / 시야에 / 유일하게 대략 12살의 여자아이가 있었다 / 눈을 붕대로 덮은 채로 / 그리고 조심스럽게 이끌어지고 있었다 / 화단사이로 / 작은 남자아이에 의해 / 그녀는 멈췄다 / 그리고 불가피하게 물었다 / 누가 왔는지 / 그리고 그는 / 묘사하는 것 같았다 / 나를 / 그녀에게

의역 해석

시야에는 아무도 없었지만 유일하게 눈을 붕대로 감은 대략 12살의 여자아이가 작은 남자아이에 의해 화단사이로 조심스럽게 이끌어지고 있었다. 그녀는 멈춰서 누가 왔는지 물었고 그는 나를 그녀에게 묘사하는 것 같았다.

56. Speaking / of marrying / creativity and business, / I've discovered / that a rock star and a brain surgeon / have something in common. / It's not that either one / would be particularly good at / the other's craft (and I'm not sure which crossover would produce the more disastrous results), but rather that each one / is capable of performing / his craft / brilliantly, / and generating / huge sums of money, / without the need for any financial skills.

직독직해 해석

말하자면 / 결합하는 것에 대해 / 창의성과 사업을, / 전 발견했다 / 락스타와 뇌 외과의사들이 / 공통점을 가지고 있다는 것을. / 둘 다가 / 잘 하기 때문이 아니라 / 서로의 기술을 / (난 어떤 교차가 더 재앙적인 결과를 만들어낼지 확실하지 않다), / 각각의 것이 / 수행할 수 있기 때문이다 / 그의 능력을 / 훌륭하게, / 그리고 만들어낼 수 있다. / 많은 양의 돈을 / 어떤 금전적 기술에 대한 필요도 없이.

의역 해석

창의성과 사업을 결합하는 것에 대해 말하자면, 전 뇌외과 의사와 락스타가 공통점을 가지고 있다는 것을 발견했습니다. 둘 다 서로의 기술을 잘 하기 때문이 아니라 각각의 사람들이 어떤 금전적 기술에 대한 필요도 없이 그의 능력을 훌륭하게 수행할 수 있고 많은 양의 돈을 벌 수 있기 때문이다.

57. Furthermore, / given the time and money / required to get / a PhD / and its uncertain economic returns, / it is clear / that most of us / pursue / an academic career / for idealistic, / rather than pragmatic, reasons.

직독직해 해석

더욱이 / 시간과 돈을 고려해볼 때 / 필요로 되어지는 / 얻기 위해 / 박사학위를 / 그리고 불확실한 경제적 이득을 / 명백하다 / 우리들 중 대부분이 / 추구한다는 것은 / 학문적인 커리어를 / 이상적인 이유로 / 실질적인 이유보다는.

의역 해석

더욱이, 박사학위와 불확실한 경제적 이득을 얻기 위해 필요로 되어지는 시간과 돈을 고려해볼 때 우리들 중 대부분이 학문적 커리어를 실질적 이유보다는 이상적인 이유로 추구한다는 것은 명백하다.

58. Considering the American cultural emphasis / on greatness, / it perhaps should come as no surprise / that the genre of the tall tale / has long struck a resonant chord / in the American mind.

직독직해 해석

미국 문화의 강조를 고려해볼 때 / 엄청남에 대한, 놀라울 일이 아니다 / 거인 이야기 장르가 / 오랫동안 심금을 울렸다는 것은 / 미국인들의 마음 속에.

의역 해석

위대한 것에 대한 미국의 문화적인 강조를 고려해볼 때, 사실이 아닌 허무맹랑한 이야기 장르가 미국인들의 마음 속에 오랫동안 심금을 울렸다는 것은 놀랍지 않다.

Unit 4 인과 관계 구문 P.98

59. What the psychologists discovered / was that most of the people / moved / far enough away from the post / so that tossing the rings / around it / was challenging / but not so difficult / as to be totally frustrating.

직독직해 해석

심리학자들이 발견한 것은 / 대부분의 사람들이 / 움직인다는 것이다 / 충분히 멀리 / 포스트로부터 / 고리를 던질 수 있도록 / 그것 주변으로 / 어렵다 / 그러나 / 꽤 어렵지는 않다 / 완전히 좌절감을 줄만큼

의역 해석

심리학자들은 대부분의 사람들이 그것 주변으로 고리를 던지는 것이 좌절감을 줄 만큼 완전히 어렵지는 않지만 꽤나 어려운 거리로 충분히 멀리 움직인다는 것을 발견했다.

60. You / may think / that moving a short distance / is so easy / that you / can do it / in no time with little effort.

직독직해 해석

너는 / 생각할지도 모른다 / 짧은 거리를 움직이는 것이 / 너무 쉬워서 / 너는 / 그것을 할 수 있다고 / 즉시 거의 어떠한 노력도 없이

의역 해석

너는 짧은 거리를 움직이는 것이 너무 쉬워서, 즉시 어떠한 노력도 없이 그것을 할 수 있다고 생각할지도 모른다.

61. The sense of sight / is so highly developed / in humans / that messages / received from other senses / are often ignored / if they conflict / with what is seen.

직독직해 해석

시각은 / 너무 많이 발달되어서 / 인간에 의해 / 메시지들이 / 다른 감각으로부터 받은 / 종종 무시된다 / 만약에 그들이 상충한다면 / 보여지는 것들과

의역 해석

시각은 인간에 의해 너무 많이 발달되어서 다른 감각으로부터 받은 메시지들이 보여지는 것들과 상충한다면 종종 무시된다.

62. Public concern / is so great / in some countries / that food companies / are ending / the use of GM crops / altogether.

직독직해 해석

대중들의 걱정은 / 너무 대단해서 / 몇몇 나라들에서 / 음식 회사들은 / 중단하고 있다 / GM 작물을 사용하는 것을 / 모두

의역 해석

몇몇 나라들에서 대중들의 걱정이 너무 대단해서 음식 회사들은 GM작물을 사용하는 것을 모두 중단하고 있다.

63. Afterimages / can produce / simultaneous contrast effects. / If these / are illusory colors, / they / nonetheless do / much of the work / of real colors, / so much so / that one / can set up / situations / in which afterimage colors / will be taken / to be the colors / of particular physical objects / or of the light / that illuminates / them.

직독직해 해석

잔상은 / 만들어낼 수 있다 / 동시의 대조 효과를. / 만약 이러한 것들이 / 허구의 색상이라고 해도, / 그것들은 / 그럼에도 불구하고 한다 / 많은 일을 / 실제 색의, / 너무나도 그러해서 / 사람은 / 설치할 수 있다 / 상황을 / 잔상의 색깔들이 / 여겨질 수 있는 / 색이라고 / 특정한 물리적 물체의 / 또는 빛의 / 밝혀주는 / 그것들을(물체들을).

의역 해석

잔상은 동시 대조 효과를 만들어낼 수 있다. 이러한 것들이 허구의 색상이라고 해도 그것들은 실제 색상의 많은 일을 한다. 너무 많이 해서 사람은 잔상의 색이 특정한 물리적 물체들이나 그것을 밝혀주는 빛의 색이라고 여겨질 수 있는 상황을 만들어낼 수 있다.

64. Teenagers' behavior / changes / when they realize / others are too busy / with their own lives / to watch them.

직독직해 해석

십대들의 행동은 / 변한다 / 그들이 깨달을 때 / 다른 사람들이 너무 바빠서 / 그들 자신의 삶에 / 그들을 볼 수 없다는 것을

의역 해석

십대들의 행동은 다른 사람들이 그들 자신의 삶에 너무 바빠서 그들을 볼 수 없다는 것을 깨달을 때 십대들의 행동은 변한다.

65. People / often sell / old record albums, bottles, and books / for pennies / only to see / them / resold / for tens or hundreds of dollars / as parts of larger collections.

직독직해 해석

사람들은 / 종종 판다 / 오래된 레코드 앨범들 , 병들 , 책들을 / 푼돈에 / 그러나 본다 / 그것들이 / 되팔리는 것을 / 수십 수백 달러에 / 큰 수집품의 일부로서

의역 해석

사람들은 종종 오래된 레코드 앨범들, 병들, 책들을 싼 값에 팔지만 그것들이 큰 수집품의 일부로서 수십 수백달러에 되팔리는 것을 본다.

66. One of the forces / that drive evolution / is constant competition / among species, / in the course of which / one species / gains / temporary advantages / through an evolutionary innovation, / only to be overtaken / by a counter-innovation.

직독직해 해석

요소들 중 하나는 / 진화를 이끄는 / 끊임없는 경쟁이다 / 종들 사이에 / 그러한 것들의 과정에서 / 한 종들은 / 얻는다 / 일시적인 이점을 / 진화적인 혁신을 통해 / 그러나 따라잡히게 된다 / 다른 종들의 혁신에 의해

의역 해석

진화를 이끄는 요소들 중 하나는 끊임없는 경쟁이다. 그러한 경쟁의 과정에서 한 종들은 진화적인 혁신을 통해 일시적인 이점을 얻지만 다른 종들의 혁신에 의해 따라잡히게 된다.

67. In much of social science, / evidence / is used / only to affirm / a particular theory / — to search for the positive instances / that uphold it.

직독직해 해석

많은 사회과학 분야에서 / 증거는 / 사용된다 / 오로지 확인하기 위해서 / 특정한 이론을 / 긍정적인 예시들을 찾기 위해 / 그것을 뒷받침하는

의역 해석

많은 사회과학 분야에서 증거는 오로지 특정한 이론을 확인하기 위해서 사용된다. —뒷받침하는 긍정적인 예시들을 찾기 위해서

68. Scientists / have analyzed / satellite images, / never to give answers / to what caused the eruption.

직독직해 해석

과학자들은 / 분석해왔다 / 위성사진들을 / 그러나 답을 주지 못했다 / 어떤 것이 폭발을 야기 시켰는지에 대한

의역 해석

과학자들은 위성사진들을 분석해왔지만 어떤 것이 폭발을 야기 시켰는지에 대한 답을 주지 못했다.

Unit 5 ~하자마자 구문 P.104

69. Upon entering a record store, one encounters a wide variety of genres from easy listening to jazz and classical music.

직독직해 해석

음반가게에 들어가자마자 / 한 사람은 / 마주친다 / 넓고 다양한 장르를 / 쉽게 듣는 것으로부터 재즈와 클래식까지

의역 해석

음반가게에 들어가자마자 한 사람은 쉽게 듣는 음악에서부터 재즈와 클래식까지 넓고 다양한 장르를 마주친다.

70. Hardly had I come into contact with him / when I determined / to get to know him well. / Never in my life / have I been so strongly and immediately attracted / to any man, / before or since.

직독직해 해석

내가 그와 만나게 되자마자 / 나는 결심했다 / 그를 더 잘 알기로 / 내 삶에서/ 한번도 이렇게 강력하고 즉석에서 끌린 적이 없었다 / 어느 남자에게도 / 여태까지

의역 해석

그와 만나게 되자마자 나는 그를 더 잘 알기로 결심했다. 나는 여태까지 어느 남자에게도 이렇게 강력하고 즉석에서 끌린 적이 없었다.

71. Health-conscious Americans / increasingly find / themselves / confused by contradictory advice. / No sooner do they learn / the results of one study / than they hear / of one with opposite message.

직독직해 해석

건강에 관심이 있는 미국인들은 / 점차 생각한다 / 그들 스스로가 / 혼란스럽다고 / 모순된 조언 때문에 / 그들이 배우자마자 / 한 연구의 결과를 / 그들은 듣는다 / 반대의 메시지를

의역 해석

건강에 관심이 있는 미국인들은 모순된 조언 때문에 그들 스스로가 혼란스럽다고 느낀다. 그들이 한 연구의 연구 결과를 배우자마자 그들은 반대의 메시지를 듣는다.

72. As soon as you start to speak to someone else, your language serves as an instantly recognizable badge of your group identity.

직독직해 해석

당신이 시작하자마자 / 누군가에게 말하는 것을 / 너의 언어는 / 역할을 한다 / 즉시 인식할 수 있는 징표로서의 / 너의 그룹 정체성의

의역 해석

당신이 누군가에게 말하는 것을 시작하자마자 너의 언어는 너의 그룹 정체성을 즉시 인식할 수 있는 징표로서의 역할을 한다.

Unit 6 부정 구문 P.108

73. Scientific and professional policy design / does not necessarily escape / the pitfalls of degenerative politics.

직독직해 해석

과학적이고 전문적인 정책 디자인은 / 반드시 피하는 것은 아니다 / 퇴보하는 정책의 위험성을

의역 해석

과학적이고 전문적인 정책 디자인은 퇴보하는 정책의 위험성을 반드시 피하는 것은 아니다.

74. Not all children of successful people / become successful themselves.

직독직해 해석

성공한 사람들의 모든 아이들은 / 스스로 성공하는 것은 아니다

의역 해석

성공한 사람들의 모든 아이들이 스스로 성공하는 것은 아니다.

75. No matter how good your product is, / remember / that perfection of an existing product / is not necessarily the best investment / one can make.

직독직해 해석

아무리 너의 제품이 좋을지라도 / 기억해라 / 현재 제품의 완벽함이 / 최고의 투자는 아니라는 것을 / 한 사람이 할 수 있는

의역 해석

아무리 너의 제품이 좋을지라도 현재 제품의 완벽함이 반드시 당신이 할 수 있는 최고의 투자는 아니라는 것을 기억해라.

76. Benjamin Bloom, / an education psychologist, / wrote / in 1985 / that none of his students / achieved their goals / without a supportive environment / and a long and intensive period of training.

직독직해 해석

Benjamin Bloom은 / 교육 심리학자인 / 썼다 / 1985년에 / 그의 학생들 중 어느 누구도 / 성취하지 못했다고 / 그들의 목표를 / 지지하는 환경 없이는 / 길고 강력한 긴 기간의 훈련 없이는

의역 해석

지지하는 환경과 긴 기간 동안의 강한 훈련이 있어야 목표를 성취할 수 있다고 교육 심리학자인 Benjamin Bloom이 썼다.

77. There is no basis / for believing / that technology / will not cause / new and unanticipated problems / while solving the problems / that it previously produced.

직독직해 해석

어떠한 근거도 없다 / 믿는 것에 대한 / 기술이 / 야기시키지 않을 거라는 / 새롭고 예기치 못한 문제들을 / 문제들을 해결 하면서 / 이것이 이전에 만들어낸

의역 해석

기술은 이전에 있던 문제들을 해결하면서 새롭고 예기치 못한 문제들을 야기시킬 것이다.

78. The black serpent, chaos, / has / a white dot / in its head. / The white serpent, order, / has / a black dot / in its head. / This is because chaos and order / are interchangeable, / as well as eternally juxtaposed. / There is nothing / so certain / that it / cannot vary.

직독직해 해석

혼란인 검은 뱀은 / 가지고 있다 / 하얀색 점을 / 머리에. / 질서인 하얀색 뱀은 / 가지고 있다 / 검은 점을 / 머리에. / 이것은 질서와 혼란이 / 서로 교환가능하기 때문이다 / 영원히 서로 병치되어(대립되어) 있을 뿐만 아니라. / 어떤 것도 없다 / 매우 확실한 / 이것이 / 달라질 수 없을 정도로

의역 해석

혼란을 상징하는 검은 뱀은 머리에 하얀색 점을 가지고 있다. 질서를 상징하는 하얀색 뱀은 머리게 검은 점을 가지고 있다. 이것은 질서와 혼란이 서로 영원히 병행할 수 있을 뿐만 아니라 서로 교환 가능하기 때문이다. 달라질 수 없을 정도로 매우 확실한 그 어떤 것도 없다.(어떤 것이든 모두 바뀔 수 있다.)

79. We / must remember / that art / is not necessarily beauty: / that cannot be said too often.

직독직해 해석

우리는 / 기억해야만한다 / 예술이 / 반드시 아름답지는 않다는 것을 / 즉 이것은 아무리 자주 말해도 지나치지 않다.

의역 해석

우리는 예술이 반드시 아름답지는 않다는 것을 기억해야만 한다. 이것은 아무리 자주 말해도 지나치지 않다.

80. It cannot be too often repeated / that it is not helps / but obstacles, / not facilities / but difficulties / that make men great.

직독직해 해석

아무리 자주 반복되어져도 지나치지 않다 / 도움이 아니라 / 장애가 / 편의가 아니라 / 어려움이 / 인간을 위대하게 만든다는 것은

의역 해석

도움이 아니라 장애가, 편의가 아니라 어려움이 인간을 위대하게 만든다는 것은 아무리 자주 반복되어 말해져도 지나치지 않다.

81. The only thing in the world / which one can never receive or give too much / is love. One / does not spoil / children / by giving too much, / but by giving them too little.

직독직해 해석

세계에서 유일한 것은 / 한 사람이 아무리 많이 받거나 줘도 지나치지 않는 것은 / 사랑이다 / 한 사람은 / 망칠 수 없다 / 아이들을 / 너무 많이 줌으로써 / 그러나 너무 적게 줌으로써

의역 해석

한 사람이 아무리 많이 받거나 줘도 지나치지 않는 세계에서 유일한 것은 사랑이다. 한 사람은 사랑을 너무 많이 줌으로써 아이들을 망칠 수는 없지만 너무 적게 줌으로써 아이들을 망칠 수 있다.

82. One of the commodities in life / that most people / can't get enough of / is compliments.

직독직해 해석

삶에서 상품들 중에 하나는 / 대부분의 사람들이 / 충분히 얻을 수 없는 / 칭찬이다

의역 해석

대부분의 사람들이 아무리 받아도 충분하지 않는 상품들 중에 하나는 칭찬이다.

83. Many people / believe / that it is critical / to share similar, / if not identical, / beliefs and values / with someone / with whom they have a relationship. / While this / may seem preferable, / it is far from mandatory.

직독직해 해석

많은 사람들은 / 믿는다 / 중요하다고 / 공유하는 것이 / 유사한 / 설령 똑같지는 않을 지라도 / 믿음이나 가치들을 / 사람들과 / 그들이 관계를 맺고 있는 / 비록 이것이 / 선호되는 것 같을 지라도 / 이것은 절대로 의무적인 것이 아니다.

의역 해석

많은 사람들은 우리가 관계를 맺고 있는 사람들과 똑같지는 않을 지라도 비슷한 믿음이나 가치들을 공유하는 것이 중요하다고 믿지만, 이것은 절대로 의무적인 것은 아니다.

84. Health / is perhaps the most striking example / of the paradoxical combination / of smart elements and often-stupid results. / We / now benefit / from vastly more access to information / on diseases, diagnoses, and treatments / on the Internet. / But this / is far from a golden age / of healthy activity or intelligence about health.

직독직해 해석

건강은 / 아마 가장 두드러지는 예시일 것이다 / 역설적인 조합의 / 똑똑한 요소와 종종 어리석은 결과들의. / 우리는 / 현재 이득을 본다 / 엄청나게 더 많은 접근으로부터 / 정보에 / 질명, 진단, 그리고 치료법에 대한 / 인터넷에 있는. 그런데 이것은 / 절대 황금시대가 아니다 / 건강한 활동 또는 건강에 대한 지식의.

의역 해석

건강은 아마 똑똑한 요소와 종종 어리석은 결과의 역설적 결합물의 가장 두드러지는 예시일 것이다. 우리는 인터넷에 있는 질명과 진단과 치료법에 대한 정보에 훨씬 더 많이 접근할 수 있는 것으로부터 이익을 보고 있다. 하지만 이 시대가 절대 건강에 대한 지식 또는 건강한 활동의 황금시대는 아니다.

85. As a matter of fact, / the sense of sin, / so far from being a cause of good life, / is quite the reverse. / It makes / a man / unhappy / and it makes him / feel inferior.

직독직해 해석

사실상 / 죄의식은 / 절대로 좋은 삶의 원인이기는커녕 / 그 반대이다 / 그것은 / 사람을 / 불행하게 만들고 / 그가 / 열등감을 느끼게 한다.

의역 해석

사실상, 죄의식은 좋은 삶의 원인이기는커녕 그 반대이다. 그것은 사람을 불행하게 만들고 열등감을 느끼게 한다.

86. My 19-year-old son / fell asleep / driving to work this morning. / He's lucky / to be alive / since his car / was damaged / beyond repair.

직독직해 해석

내 19살 아들이 / 잠에 들었다 / 아침에 일 가며 운전하면서 / 그는 운이 좋았다 / 살아서 / 왜냐하면 그의 차가 / 피해를 입었기 때문에 / 고칠 수 없을 정도로

의역 해석

아침에 내 19살 아들이 운전하면서 잠에 들었다. 그의 차는 고칠 수 없을 정도로 피해를 입었기 때문에 그가 살아있는 것은 운이 좋았다.

87. Distance learning / has recently become prominent / in the field of further education. / However, / much / about the processes / and the participants involved / is yet to be ful8ly understood.

직독직해 해석

원격교육은 / 유명해졌다 / 성인 교육 분야에서 / 그러나 / 많은 것들 / 과정에 대한 / 그리고 참가자들은 / 참여된 / 아직 충분히 이해하지는 못했다.

의역 해석

원격교육은 성인교육 시장에서 유명해졌다. 그러나 과정에 대한 많은 것들과 포함된 참가자들은 아직 충분히 이해하지는 못했다.

Unit 7 목적 구문 P.116

88. It is therefore important,/ if not essential, / to maintain / a clear focus / in undertaking advocacy or mediation / in order to ensure / that the roles / do not become blurred / and therefore potentially counterproductive.

직독직해 해석

그러므로 중요하다 / 설령 필수적이지는 않을지라도 / 유지하는 것이 / 명백한 초점을 / 지지나 중재를 착수함에 있어서 / 확실하게 하기 위해서 / 그 역할들이 / 모호해지지 않고 / 그러므로 비생산적이게 되지 않기 위해

의역 해석

그 역할들이 모호해지고 비생산적이 되는 것을 막는 것을 확실하게 하기 위해 설령 필수적이지는 않을지라도 지지나 중재를 착수함에 있어서 명확한 초점을 유지하는 것은 중요하다.

89. It was, therefore, / Important / for the viewer / to create a distance / from the actions on the stage / so as to facilitate / interpretation of the content.

직독직해 해석

따라서 / 중요하다 / 관람자들이 / 거리를 만드는 것이 / 무대의 행동으로부터 / 쉽게 하기 위해서 / 내용의 해석을

의역 해석

따라서 내용의 해석을 쉽게 하기 위해서 관람자들이 무대의 행동으로부터 거리를 두는 것이 중요하다.

90. I have been working hard / so that my family / can enjoy / an easy and convenient life.

직독직해 해석

나는 열심히 일해오고 있는 중이다 / 내 가족들이 / 즐길 수 있게 하기 위해서 / 쉽고 편리한 삶을

의역 해석

나는 내 가족들이 쉽고 편리한 삶을 즐길 수 있게 하기 위해서 열심히 일해오고 있는 중이다.

91. When you travel, / be sure / to make your budget / realistic / in order that you / can be confident / that you / will be able to pay / for all aspects of the trip.

직독직해 해석

너가 여행을 할 때 / 확실하게 해라 / 너의 예산을 / 현실적으로 하는 것을 / 너가 / 자신 있을 수 있기 위해 / 너가 / 지불할 수 있다는 것을 / 여행의 모든 비용에 대해

의역 해석

너가 여행을 할 때 여행의 모든 비용에 대해 지불할 수 있다는 자신이 있을 수 있기 위해서, 너의 예산을 현실적으로 하는 것을 확실하게 해라.

92. Some students with disease / were found / to have been hiding their infection / and attended / class / for days / for fear that they / should ruin their school grades.

직독직해 해석

질병을 가진 몇몇 학생들을 / 발견되었다 / 그들의 병을 숨기는 것으로 / 그리고 참석했다 / 수업에 / 며칠 동안 / 그들이 / 그들의 학교 성적을 망치지 않기 위해서

의역 해석

질병을 가진 몇몇 학생들은 자신들의 학교 성적을 망치지 않기 위해서 그들의 병을 숨기고 며칠 동안 수업에 참석하는 것으로 발견되었다.

93. Furthermore, / news-based tasks / can be used / as a context / for students / to demonstrate / their knowledge / with a view to identifying / gaps / in their understanding / or weaknesses in their ability / to make links / between related areas of learning.

직독직해 해석

더욱이, 뉴스에 기반한 일들은 / 사용될 수 있다 / 상황으로서 / 학생들이 / 입증하는 / 그들의 지식을 / 확인하려는 목적으로 / 차이를 / 그들의 이해도에 있어서 / 그리고 약점을 / 그들의 능력에 있어서 / 연결관계를 만들 수 있는 / 배움의 관련된 분야들 사이에서

의역 해석

더욱이 뉴스에 기반한 일들은 학생들이 이해도에 있어서의 차이를 확인하고 배움의 관련 분야들 사이에서의 연결관계를 만드는 능력에 있어서의 약점을 확인하려는 목적으로 학생들이 그들의 지식을 입증하는 상황으로써 사용될 수 있다.

Unit 8 가정법 구문 P.120

94. If you / knew me well, / you / would know / that I am shameless / enough / to take all compliments / at their face value / and not to think / that they might be mere flattery.

직독직해 해석

만약 너가 / 나를 잘 안다면 / 너는 / 알 것이다 / 내가 / 뻔뻔하다는 것을 / 충분히 / 모든 칭찬을 / 있는 그대로의 가치로 / 그리고 생각하지 않을 정도로 / 그들이 / 단순히 아부일지도 모른다고

의역 해석

만약 너가 나를 잘 안다면 너는 내가 모든 칭찬을 있는 그대로 받아들일 정도로 충분히 뻔뻔하고, 그것들이 단순히 아부라고 생각하지 않는다는 것을 알 것이다.

95. If I / had told you the truth, / you / might have panicked / and none of us / would have made it.

직독직해 해석

만약 내가 / 너에게 진실을 말했더라면 / 너는 / 당황했을 것이다 / 그리고 우리중 누구도 / 그것을 성공하지 못했을 것이다

의역 해석

만약 내가 너에게 진실을 말했더라면 너는 당황했을 것이고 우리 중 누구도 그것을 성공하지 못했을 것이다.

96. The domestic oil, / natural gas, / or steel industry / may require / protection / due to its importance to national defense. / If it were not for protection, / such industries / might be weakened / by foreign competition.

직독직해 해석

국내 오일 / 천연가스 / 또는 철근 산업은 / 필요로 할지도 모른다 / 보호를 / 그것의 국가 방어에 대한 중요성 때문에 / 보호가 없으면 / 그러한 산업들은 / 약화될 것이다 / 해외와의 경쟁에 의해

의역 해석

국내 오일, 천연가스, 철근 산업은 국가 방어에 대한 중요성 때문에 보호를 필요로 할지도 모른다. 보호가 없으면 그러한 산업들은 해외와의 경쟁에 의해 약화될 것이다.

97. For instance, / social order / is maintained / only on the condition / that people repress / their aggressive instincts and tendencies. / However, / for Freud, / this repression / takes an intolerably heavy toll / on human psychology. / Humans / would not be able to handle / this repression / of their instincts / were it not for some sort of psychological compensation / to relieve / the pressure.

직독직해 해석

예를 들어, / 사회적 질서는 / 유지된다 / 오로지 조건에서만 / 사람들이 / 억압하는 / 그들의 공격적 본능과 경향을. / 그러나, / Freud에겐, / 이 억압은 / 엄청난 대가를 치르게 한다 / 인간의 심리에. / 인간들은 / 다룰 수 없을 것이다 / 이 억압을 / 그들의 본능에 대한 / 어느 정도의 심리적 보상이 없으면 / 완화시켜줄 수 있는 / 그 압박을.

의역 해석

예를 들어, 사회적 질서는 오로지 사람들이 그들의 공격적 본능과 경향을 억압하는 상황에서만 유지된다. 그러나 Freud는 이 억압은 인간에게 엄청난 피해를 준다고 본다. 만약 이 압박을 완화시켜줄 수 있는 어느정도의 심리적 보상이 없으면 인간들은 이 본능에 대한 억압을 해결할 수 없을 것이다.

98. If chaos / that makes everything uncertain / should distract / our society, / a leader / is expected / to restore / normality / immediately.

직독직해 해석

혼란들 / 모든 것을 불확실하게 만드는 / 방해한다면 / 우리의 사회를 / 지도자는 / 기대되어진다 / 복구하도록 / 정상상태를 / 즉시

의역 해석

모든 것을 불확실하게 만드는 혼란들이 우리 사회를 방해한다면, 지도자들은 정상 상태를 즉시 복구하도록 기대되어진다.

99. It is vital / that all students and staff / know / what to do / should we / face a wildfire.

직독직해 해석

중요하다 / 모든 학생들과 관계자들이 / 아는 것은 / 무엇을 해야 하는지를 / 혹시라도 우리가 / 산불을 마주친다면

의역 해석

모든 학생들과 관계자들이 혹시라도 산불을 마주친다면, 무엇을 해야 하는지를 아는 것은 중요하다.

100. A quicksand / may look like normal sand, / but were you to step on it, / the pressure / from your foot / would cause / the sand / to act / more like a liquid / and you'd sink right in.

직독직해 해석

유사는 / 보통의 모래처럼 보인다 / 그러나 혹시라도 너가 그것을 밟는다면 / 압력은 / 너의 발로부터의 / 초래할 것이다 / 모래로 하여금 / 작용하도록 / 액체처럼 / 너는 그것에 빠질 것이다

의역 해석

유사는 보통의 모래처럼 보이지만 혹시 너가 그것을 밟는다면 너의 발로부터의 압력이 모래로 하여금 액체처럼 작용하도록 할 것이고 너는 그것에 빠질 것이다.

101. We / tend to take pride / in our rationality / and feel / a bit ashamed / of our emotions, / as if rationality / were more likely to be right / and the emotions / commensurately / apt to be wrong.

직독직해 해석

우리는 / 자신감을 가지는 경향이 있다 / 우리의 이성에 / 그리고 느끼는 경향이 있다 / 조금 부끄럽게 / 우리의 감정에 / 마치 이성은 / 옳을 가능성이 높고 / 감정은 / 같은 비율로 / 틀릴 가능성이 높다고

의역 해석

우리는 마치 감정은 옳을 가능성이 높고 감정은 틀릴 가능성이 높다며 우리의 이성에 자신감을 가지고 감정을 조금 부끄럽게 느끼는 경향이 있다.

102. We / value / sight / above all things, / and fortunate / indeed should we / be could we / exchange / our imperfect vision / for sight / like that of an eagle!

직독직해 해석

우리는 / 가치를 둔다 / 시각에 / 그 무엇보다도, / 그리고 다행스러울 것이다 / 우리는 / 만약 우리가 / 바꿀 수 있다면 / 우리의 완전하지 못한 시야를 / 시야로 / 독수리의 시야와 같은.

의역 해석

우리는 그 무엇보다도 시각에 가치를 둔다. 그리고 만약 우리가 우리의 완벽하지 못한 시각을 독수리의 시각과 같은 것으로 바꿀 수 있다면 정말 다행스러울 것이다.

Unit 9 It~that 강조 구문 P.126

103. It is often thinking / of so many things / and consideration of so many doubts / that result in / the difficulty / to reach and act / on a simple decision.

직독직해 해석

종종 생각하는 것은 / 너무 많은 것을 / 너무 많은 의심들에대한 생각은 / 야기시킨다 / 어려움을 / 도달하고 행동하는 것의 / 간단한 결정에

의역 해석

종종 너무 많은 것을 생각하고 너무 많은 의심들에 대해 생각하는 것은 간단한 결정에 도달하고 행동하는데에 어려움을 야기시킨다.

104. It is only when we / let / our minds / wander / that we / make unexpected connections / between things / that we / did not realize / were connected. / This / can help / you / solve / problems / that previously seemed to be unsolvable.

직독직해 해석

오로지 우리가 / 우리의 마음이 / 돌아다니게 할 때에만 / 우리는 / 예상치 못한 연결관계를 지을 수 있다 / 것들 사이에서 / 우리가 깨닫지 못하는 / 연결되어 있다고 / 이것은 / 도울 수 있다 / 당신이 / 해결하는 것을 / 문제를 / 이전에는 해결할 수 없을 것처럼 보였던.

의역 해석

오로이 우리가 우리의 마음이 돌아다니게 할 때에만 우리는 우리가 연결되어있다고 깨닫지 못했던 것들 사이의 연결관계를 지을 수 있다. 이것은 당신이 과거에 해결 불가능해보였던 문제들을 해결하는 것을 도와줄 수 있다.

105. It is believed / that brightness of the Sun / can be predicted / theoretically.

직독직해 해석

사람들은 믿는다 / 태양의 밝기가 / 예측될 수 있다고 / 이론적으로

의역 해석

사람들은 이론적으로 태양의 밝기를 예측할 수 있다는 것을 믿는다.

106. This kind of decision making / is the result / of an authentic question / generated / by the learner / on the basis / of a genuine need / to know / and is one / that inevitably requires / more complex thinking. / It is / the search for meaning / that organizes / actor-centered questions / and encourages / the use of higher-order functions.

직독직해 해석

이러한 종류의 의사 결정은 / 결과이다 / 진짜 문제의 / 만들어지는 / 학습자에 의해 / 기초로 하여 / 진짜 필요에 / 알아야 할 / 그리고 질문이다. / 불가피하게 필요로하는 / 더 복잡한 생각을. / 의미 탐색은 / 정리한다 / 행위자 중심의 문제를 / 그리고 장려한다 / 더 고차적인 기능을.

의역 해석

이러한 종류의 의사결정은 학습자가 진정으로 알아야 할 필요성에 기초하여 만들어 낸 진정한 질문의 결과로서 불가피하게 좀 더 복잡한 생각을 필요로 하는 질문이다. 배우 중심의 질문을 정리하고 고차적인 기능의 사용을 장려하는 의미 탐색이다.

107. It is not just the newness of contemporary literature / that makes it different, / but also the context / in which it is written and received, / something which gives it / a very interesting edge / over the literature of the past.

직독직해 해석

현대 문학의 새로움 뿐만아니라 / 이것을 다르게 만들어 줄 / 상황이다 / 이것이 쓰여지고 받아들여지는 / 주는 / 이것에게 주는 것이다 / 매우 흥미로운 이점을 / 과거의 문학보다

의역 해석

현대 문학의 새로움이 현대문학을 다르게 만들어줄 뿐만 아니라 과거의 문학 보다 매우 흥미로운 이점을 주는 그 안에서 현대문학이 쓰여지고 받아들여지는 상황 또한 그것을 다르게 만든다.

108. It is likely / that some children and young people / have no idea / of what needs to be changed / in their life. / The concept / of having / power and control / over our lives / to effect / change / is a fairly abstract one, / and goal setting / is not something / we / typically encourage / young people / to do, / aside from reaching / academic goals / or passing / exams.

직독직해 해석

가능성이 있다 / 몇몇 아이들과 젊은 사람들이 / 모를 / 무엇이 바뀌어야 하는지를 / 그들의 삶에서. / 개념은 / 가진다는 / 힘과 통제력을 / 우리의 삶에 / 야기시키기 위해 / 변화를 / 꽤 추상적인 개념이다, 그리고 목표 설정은 / 우리가 / 보통 장려하는 것이 아니다 / 젊은 사람들이 / 하도록, / 도달하는 것을 제외하고 / 학문적 목표 / 또는 통과하는 것을 제외하고 / 시험에

의역 해석

몇몇 아이들과 젊은 사람들은 그들의 삶에서 무엇이 바뀌어야 하는지를 모를 가능성이 있다. 변화를 야기시키기 위해 자신의 삶에 힘과 통제력을 가진다는 개념은 꽤 추상적인 개념이고, 학문적 목표에 도달하거나 시험에 통과하는 것을 제외하고 목표 설정은 우리가 젊은 사람들이 하도록 장려하는 것이 아니다.

109. It turns out / that it's the sense of control / that matters, / even more so / than what you / actually do. / If you / have / confidence / that you / can impact / a situation, / it / will be less stressful. / In contrast, / a low sense of control / may very well be the most stressful thing / in the universe.

직독직해 해석

통제력에 대한 감각이 / 중요하다고 입증되었다, / 훨씬 더 그렇다고 / 당신이 / 실제로 하는 것 보다. / 만약 당신이 / 가지고 있다면 / 자신감을 / 당신이 / 영향을 줄 수 있다는 / 상황에, / 이것은 / 훨씬 덜 스트레스가 될 것이다. / 대조적으로, / 낮은 통제력은 / 당연하게도 가장 스트레스가 받는 것이 될 것이다 / 우주에서.

의역 해석

당신이 실제로 뭔가 하는 것 보다 통제할 수 있다는 느낌이 중요하다고 입증되었다. 만약 당신이 상황에 영향을 줄 수 있다는 자신감을 가지고 있다면 스트레스는 훨씬 덜 해질 것이다. 대조적으로, 통제력이 낮은 것은 당연하게도 우주에서 가장 스트레스를 받는 것이 될 것이다.

110. It follows that / the most common alternative names / for digital code and hypertext / are multimedia, interactive media and digital media.

직독직해 해석

당연하다 / 가장 흔한 대안이 되는 이름들이 / 디지털 코드와 하이퍼 텍스트의 / 멀티미디어, 상호작용 미디어, 디지털 미디어 인 것은

의역 해석

디지털 코드와 하이퍼 텍스트의 가장 흔한 대안이 되는 이름들이 멀티미디어, 상호작용 미디어, 디지털 미디어라는 것은 당연하다.

111. Sometimes, / It seems that people / simply like / to try new things — / they are interested / in variety seeking, / in which the priority / is to vary / one's product experiences, / perhaps as a form of stimulation or / to avoid / being bored.

직독직해 해석

때때로 / 사람들은 / 좋아하는 것 같다 / 새로운 것을 / 그들은 / 흥미가 있다 / 다양성 추구에 / 우선순위는 / 다양화하는 것이다 / 한 사람의 상품 경험들을 / 아마도 자극의 형태로 / 또는 피하는 것이다 / 지루한 것을

의역 해석

때때로 사람들은 새로운 것을 시도하는 것을 좋아하는 것 같다. 즉, 그들은 다양성을 추구하는 것에 흥미가 있고 그 안에서 우선순위는 아마도 자극이라는 형태로 상품 경험들을 다양화하는 것이나 지루한 것을 피하는 것이다.

112. It appears that measures / that protect drivers / from the consequences / of bad driving / encourage / bad driving.

직독직해 해석

방안들 / 운전자들을 보호해주는 / 결과로부터 / 나쁜 운전의 / 격려하는 것 같다/ 나쁜 운전을

의역 해석

나쁜 운전의 결과로부터 운전자들을 보호해주는 방안들은 오히려 나쁜 운전을 장려하는 것 같다.

113. It used to be that a photographer / would look / and then shoot, / taking time / to compose the image / and look for / important relationships / within the scene / before tripping the shutter, / even if it / was as rapid-fire / as street photography.

직독직해 해석

사진사는 / 보고 / 그러고 찍곤했다 / 시간을 들이면서 / 이미지를 구성하는 / 그리고 찾으면서 / 중요한 관계들을 / 그 장면 안에서 / 셔터를 누르기 전에 / 비록 그것이 / 빠르게 찍을지라도 / 길거리 사진술처럼

의역 해석

사진사는 비록 그것이 길거리 사진술처럼 빠르게 찍을 지라도 셔터를 누르기 전에 그 장면 안에서 중요한 관계들을 찾고 이미지를 구성하는 시간을 들이면서 먼저 본 다음에 사진을 찍곤 했다.

Unit 10 특이한 구문

P.132

114. Most organic farmers / have no choice but to rely on / chemicals / as necessary supplements / to their operations.

직독직해 해석

대부분의 유기농 농부들은 / 의존할 수밖에 없었다 / 화학 물질에 / 필수적인 보충제로서 / 그들의 농사에 있어서

의역 해석

대부분의 유기농 농부들은 그들의 농사에 있어서 필수적인 보충제로서 화학물질에 의존할 수밖에 없었다.

115. Uneducated people / who could not read / the book / that was a dead language / to them, / saw / nothing but all manner of pretty pictures / in it.

직독직해 해석

교육받지 않은 사람들은 / 읽을 수 없는 / 책을 / 읽을 수 없는 언어로 된 / 그들에게 / 본다 / 오직 온갖 종류의 이쁜 그림들만 / 그안의

의역 해석

책을 읽을 수 없는 교육받지 않은 사람들은 책 안의 온갖종류의 이쁜 그림들만 본다.

116. The traditional Chinese manner / of producing / tea / was anything but industrial / and had remained unchanged / for hundreds of years.

직독직해 해석

전통적인 중국의 방식은 / 만드는 / 차를 / 절대 산업적이지 않았고 / 변하지 않는채로 있었다 / 수백년 동안.

의역 해석

전통적인 중국의 차를 만드는 방식은 절대 산업적이지 않았고 수백년동안 변하지 않는 채로 있었다.

117. At times, / coaches / are so focused / on helping athletes improve / that they / take good performance efforts / for granted.

직독직해 해석

때때로 / 코치들은 / 너무 집중을 해서 / 운동선수들이 향상되는 것을 돕는데 / 그들은 / 좋은 수행하려는 노력을 / 당연하게 여긴다

의역 해석

때때로코치들은 운동선수들이 향상되는 것을 돕는데 너무 집중해서 그들이 좋은 수행을 위해 노력하는 것을 당연하게 여긴다.

118. We / take it for granted / that people / of different ages / behave / differently.

직독직해 해석

우리는 / 당연하게 여긴다 / 사람들이 / 다양한 나이의 / 행동한다는 것을 / 다르게

의역 해석

우리는 다양한 나이의 사람들이 다르게 행동한다는 것을 당연하게 여긴다.

119. Chances / are everything / in the store / from the layout and lighting to the music and even the smells / has been organized / to help / shape / your shopping experience — and to open / your wallet.

직독직해 해석

아마도 모든 것들 / 가게에 있는 / 배열과 불빛부터 음악과 심지어 냄새까지도 / 조직되었다 / 돕기위해 / 너의 쇼핑 경험을 / 그리고 열기 위해서 / 너의 지갑을

의역 해석

아마도 배열과 불빛부터 음악과 심지어 냄새까지 가게에 있는 모든 것들은 너의 지갑을 열기 위해, 너의 쇼핑 경험을 돕기 위해 조직되었을 것이다.

120. Estimates are that 90 percent of the world's data / has been created / in the last five years. / We're all / drowning / in information, / a reality / that makes even the simplest decisions / — where to eat, / which health plan to sign up for, / which coffee maker to buy — / more complicated.

직독직해 해석

아마도 90퍼센트의 세계의 데이터는 / 만들어져왔다 / 지난 오년 동안 / 우리 모두는 / 익사하고 있다 / 정보에 / 즉 현실이다 / 심지어 가장 단순한 결정들 조차도 / 어디에서 먹을지 / 어떤 건강 계획에 등록을 할지 / 어떤 커피 메이커를 살지 / 더 복잡하게 만드는

의역 해석

아마도 90퍼센트의 세계의 데이터는 지난 오년동안 만들어져 왔다. 우리 모두는 어디에서 먹을지, 어떤 건강계획에 등록을 할지, 어떤 커피 메이커를 살지같은 가장 단순한 결정들 조차도 더 복잡하게 만드는 현실이라는 정보에 익사하고 있다.

121. "Once you've started, / it / can take just six weeks / to see / an improvement of up to 20 percent / in your muscle capabilities," / says Dr. Ward.

직독직해 해석

일단 당신이 시작하고 나면 / 6주가 걸린다 / 보는 것이 / 20퍼센트 까지의 향상을 / 당신 근육의 힘에 있어서 / Dr. Ward.가 말했다

의역 해석

Dr. Ward.는 일단 당신이 시작하고 나면 당신 근육의 힘에 있어서 20퍼센트까지의 향상을 보는 것이 6주가 걸린다고 말했다.

memo

memo

memo

memo

memo

이것이 구문이다!

2021년 3월 10일 2판 1쇄 발행

저 자 이 종 현

발행인 남 승 우

발행처 도서출판 상尙 학學 당堂

서울특별시 동작구 사당로9가길 6

TEL : 02) 595-1692~4

FAX : 02) 595-1394

E-mail : namdoo6@unitel.co.kr

신고 : 2-155호 (1968. 11. 29)

정가 25,000원

ISBN 978-89-6587-211-5 03740

〈디자인〉 오름 스튜디오(o.rm studio)